INDIAN
BASKET
WEAVING

INDIAN BASKET WEAVING

by the
Navajo School of Indian Basketry

DOVER PUBLICATIONS, INC.
New York

Published in Canada by General Publishing Company, 30 Lesmill Road, Don Mills, Toronto, Ontario.
Published in the United Kingdom by Constable and Company, Ltd., 10 Orange Street, London WC 2.

This Dover edition, first published in 1971, is an unabridged republication of the work originally published by Whedon & Spreng Co., Los Angeles, in 1903.

International Standard Book Number: 0-486-22616-6
Library of Congress Catalog Card Number: 72-179789

Manufactured in the United States of America
Dover Publications, Inc.
180 Varick Street
New York, N.Y. 10014

CONTENTS.

"Baskets are the Indian Woman's poems;
the shaping of them her sculpture. They
wove into them the story of their life and love."

The Weaving of Them Today is as Much of an Art as Ever

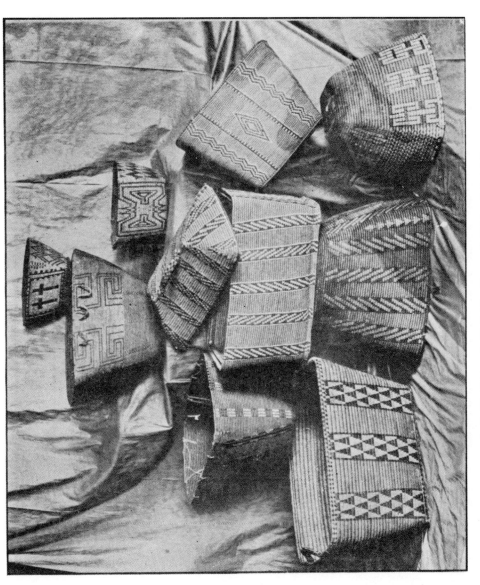

A Collection of Baskets From British Columbia.

Yokut Basket, With Interesting Design of St. Andrew's Cross.

INTRODUCTION.

The following instructions are given for those interested in the study and preservation of our American basketry. And the interest taken by all true lovers of the ancient art in the baskets woven and used for centuries by the American Indians, has been revived, and the fascinating possibilities of investigating these æsthetic elements of a rapidly vanishing race, and industry, involve a vast amount of culture study, which cannot be lightly passed as unimportant.

The lost art of Indian basketry is being revived, and those who have the knowledge necessary to correctly weave the *long* forgotten and intricate designs are securing almost fabulous prices for their work.

Indian basketry has taught us to appreciate the beauty of primitive weaving, and furnishes the most striking illustration of the wonderful patience, fertility of resource and inventive genius of the aboriginal woman in using nature's materials, roots, grasses, twigs, vines, rushes, palm-fibres, shells, and feathers, shaping them into useful and beautiful forms.

From such pitiful poverty of material would we create and decorate our commonest household articles and utensils?

The question has been asked, "What would be the civilized man of today, without the art of weaving, the soft art that surrounds his home with comfort and his life with luxuries.?"

Into the life of the Indian, baskets have entered most intimately in their domestic needs, religious and social functions. In infancy, cradled in a basket and carried on long toilsome journeys upon a mother's back, hung from some tree branch, swayed by every passing breeze, the bronze baby's earliest recollections must have been associated with baskets; baskets which filled every needed demand for cooking, burden-carrying and hoarding away of the garnered stores for winter's use.

Baskets were the Indian woman's poems, the making manifest her ideals and longings for the beautiful. We are convinced from personal observation that no one, after thoughtfully examining or doing the work, can help regarding the Indians and their wonderful productions, so filled with the unwritten poetry of a race now almost extinct, can turn away without a new interest and respect for the Indians and their baskets. Hence we feel that Indian basketry will gain appreciation, not lose, by our placing before our readers the possibilities of reeds and raphia; and while we may not have the magic of the Indian squaw in our finger tips, we are able to teach her methods and designs.

It is the purpose of this book to teach the exact weaves and designs used by the Indians for centuries past, and to neither add to or take from, their original Indian characteristics. Some of the older weaves are not now to be found outside some of the very few fine collections of baskets, and the weaves of some of the rare old baskets are now a thing of the past.

A basket made after our instructions is a real Indian basket, except for the fact that white fingers instead of brown ones fashioned it. The design was originated by the Indians and the work is performed in exactly the same manner.

In preparing these lessons it is our object to have them clear, and concise, and written exactly as a teacher would instruct a student in one of her classes.

This, with the illustrations of the different weaves and the finished baskets, cannot fail to make our instructions clear and comprehensive. In giving these lessons, we do not depart from the one idea of "pure Indian." Our teaching is authentic and the result of research and practice that, to the casual observer might seem almost impossible to obtain. Anyone who weaves the complete course of lessons given in this book will have a knowledge of basketry which cannot be obtained in any other way except by great expense in travel and a thorough study of the Indians themselves while engaged in weaving the baskets.

Indian basketry may be divided into two extremely different classes, *coiled* and *upright* weaves. These in turn include many different weaves. Coiled basketry seems to present the greatest extremes.

We have seen specimens of baskets so delicately made that they could easily pass through a lady's finger ring, and others as large or larger than a flour barrel and material one-half inch wide used for the stitching of the coils together, as for the large granary baskets. In other baskets the stitching material had been shredded or split so fine that it took nearly one hundred stitches to cover one inch of space.

Coiled basketry lends itself to the greatest variety of shapes. In form they may be perfectly flat, as in a table mat, or built up into the most exquisitely beautiful jar shapes. These stitches are capable of lending themselves to an endless variety of intricate patterns.

In the upright weaves the plain twined weaving used by different tribes seems to be the most primitive of all weaving. The large burden baskets as well as the Pomo "bam-tush" mush bowls and treasure baskets are good examples of this style of weaving. Beads, feathers and wampum entered into the decoration of these Pomo treasure baskets, making indeed wonderfully beautiful works of art. The Aleuts, Indians of the Aleutian Islands, make baskets of the twined open work weaves, while the three ply, or braided effect with its variations are found in many different baskets of different tribes.

The twined weaving of the Pomos, where the "ti" band is used for strengthening as well as beautifying the baskets, gives us some wonderful examples of really beautiful work. However, we shall speak of this again.

We hope that to all who are interested in basketry, the following instructions and illustrations of genuine Indian baskets may be welcome, and suggest an entertaining pastime, as well as an incentive to seek a broader knowledge of this beautiful art, and a better understanding of these almost hitherto unknown children of Nature.

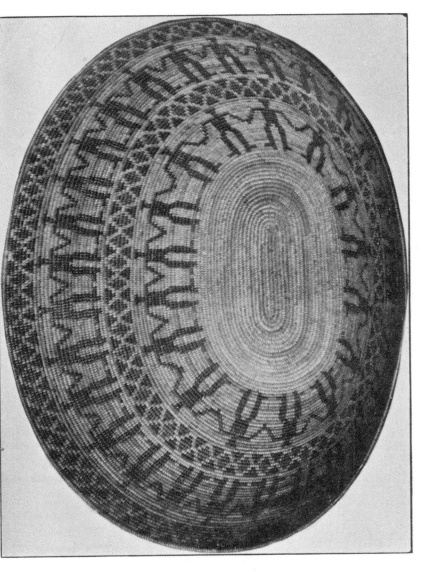

Ready For The Sun Dance,

A Rare Old Yokut Dance Basket—Color Scheme for design, Black and Indian Red, with natural colored raphia. Bottom row all black. Rattle-snake design, *whole* diamonds *red* and *half* diamonds *black.* Top row of men black with two rows of red running through upper part of body and arms.

INSTRUCTIONS FOR INDIAN BASKET WEAVING.

BY THE NAVAJO SCHOOL OF INDIAN BASKETRY.

We have endeavored to make the following description of the Navajo weave, (*and this will apply to any plain continuous coil basket,*) so clear that anyone, after a careful reading, and a thorough inspection of the accompanying illustrations, should be able to *commence* and *finish* in a correct manner baskets of their own weaving and shaping.

If it were a practical thing to do, we should most assuredly advocate the use of genuine Indian materials. But it would be impossible to obtain these in sufficient quantities and we doubt very much if the delicate fingers of the ladies could or would endure the tax put upon them. So we will use the tough, but soft and flexible raphia in lieu of the kah-hoom, reeds instead of the bundles of split willow withes, and a needle to fill the office of the ever present bone awl of the Indian woman. And with these materials proceed to weave and shape our baskets in exactly the same manner as do our darker skinned sisters.

GENERAL DIRECTIONS FOR WEAVING A CONTINUOUS COIL BASKET.

PREPARING THE REED.

Coil the reed into convenient size, tying firmly two or three times, leaving about fifteen inches uncoiled. Cover with hot water five or six inches of the uncoiled end of the reed, leaving in this water one hour to soften. When pliable, remove from water and wipe dry.

THREADING THE NEEDLE.

Always thread the needle with the end of the raphia, which has been cut from the palm. One cannot fail to recognize the right end by its darker color and somewhat hardened appearance. If the needle is not properly threaded the raphia will wear into fine threads much more quickly than otherwise. Slightly dampening the raphia in folds of a wet cloth makes it whiter and easier to work.

In regard to needles, we would suggest that should the worker contemplate weaving a number of baskets, it would be better to buy a paper of each of Nos. 18, 20 and 21, both blunt and sharp. We prefer the blunt. It is necessary to have both coarse and fine needles for the different weaves.

THE COMMENCED BASKETS.

Trim the reed with a sharp knife, one and one-half inches from the end, gradually sloping to a flat point, as in figure 1, of the illustration. Holding the reed firmly in the left hand, draw it through the fingers of the right, shaping the end into a round coil. Have the needle threaded with raphia. Hold the reed firmly in the left hand, with the forefinger upon the end of the thread, about one and one-half inches from point, carefully winding round the reed

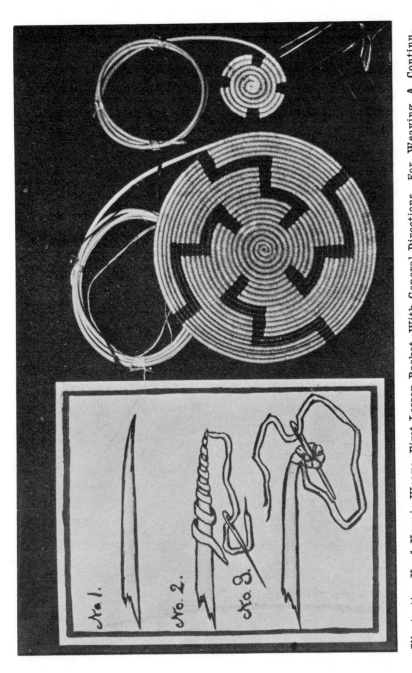

Illustration No. 1 Navajo Weave, First Lesson Basket, With General Directions For Weaving A Continuous Coil Basket.

down to the point, as illustrated in No. 2. With the right hand, using the fore-finger and thumb to force the end of reed into the smallest possible coil, sew firmly through the center as in illustration No. 3. Be sure that the reed is thoroughly covered with raphia.

The Navajo weave is really the stitching upon a continuous coil, and as the coil progresses, each stitch or weave is passed between a stitch of the coil beneath.

This passing of the thread over and under the two reeds forms the figure eight, and has often been called "the figure eight" stitch. Our illustration shows a round basket.

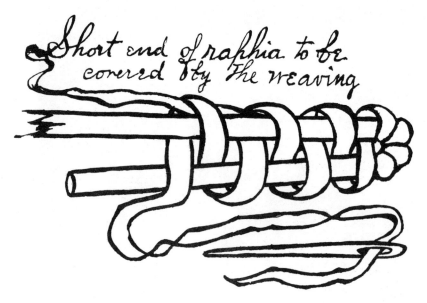

Method of Commencing Oval Basket. Navajo Weave.

This shows foundation for Klikitat overlay, Feathered or Beaded Baskets.

To commence an *oval* basket, follow directions for "preparing the reed" and after soaking in the hot water the required length of time, take out and wipe dry, measure off six or eight inches, (it will depend upon the individual taste of the worker,) and carefully bend the reed at point marked. This must be done slowly, so as not to break the reed. Do not be alarmed should it split; it can be covered by the weaving.

Hold in the *left* hand the two reeds which have been bent close together as per the cut for oval basket, keeping the *short* end underneath the long one, and the bent end toward your right hand; commence weaving by wrapping the threaded raphia twice around the *upper* reed, one inch from the bent end; hold this firmly by the forefinger of *left* hand, leaving two or three inches of the raphia, (not the needle end) to be carried along *next* the reed and *under* the weaving, to be cut off after it is firmly fastened, as per our instructions for splicing the thread.

Wrap the bent end four or five times with the raphia, enough to cover it smoothly. Now come *up between* the reeds, going *from* you *over* the long reed;

again coming up between the reeds *toward* you. Now it is the under or short reed which will receive a stitch by coming up *between* the reeds *toward* you, and now again going *over* the long reed *from* you. So continue until the *two* reeds are covered and you are ready to curve the long reed around the short one. Draw your thread firmly and do not let your reeds spread apart, but hold them closely and firmly together; so much depends upon this. Continue weaving as per our instructions for the Navajo round coiled basket, forming the figure eight stitch.

SPLICING THE THREAD.

In commencing to use a new needleful of raphia, hold the reed in the left hand with the forefinger pressed firmly on the ends of both old and new thread and wind the new thread closely over the reed and the old thread. Then proceed to weave or stitch as before, covering both old and new thread. When suf-

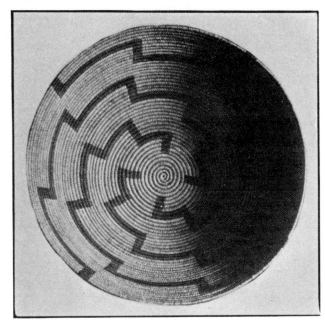

Finished Lesson Basket of Navajo Weave.

ficiently covered to hold firmly, cut off the ends of threads and continue weaving.

TO INTRODUCE COLOR.

To introduce color, thread the needle with raphia of the color desired and proceed in the same manner as described in the preceding paragraph, carrying the natural raphia along the reed, covering both by weaving. In introducing the colors in the working out of different designs, do not cut the threads in changing from one to the other, but carry them along with, and next to the reed, and cover with weaving. In all Indian designs, stitches are not counted as is generally done in our following out of geometrical designs, but the design must be filled in solid and may take more or less of the stitches, according to size of thread. And it is well to take into consideration the fact that the coils of reed are covered *twice*. Unless one does remember this, they are apt to be puzzled at first when weaving in the design. For instance, you think your design finished, or all of a certain color has been woven in, and when the next row of weaving shows a mistake or perhaps has cut off the finishing points of a border, please do not be discouraged but remember that the reeds are covered *twice*.

DESIGN.

Nearly all of the Indian designs are capable of geometrical division. A practical and easy way to arrive at this division is to place your commenced basket upon a paper, mark around it, cut out the circle, divide the paper by folding into the required divisions, marking these with pencil upon the basket.

Indian basketry differs from many other kinds of decorative work; one does not count stitches, but the idea is to fill space in a smooth, neat manner. If, for instance, you desired a band of little men for a "man basket," you would cut out of paper the required number, sizes and shapes, then proceed to weave those shapes upon your basket, using the pattern for a measurement, filling in the required spaces, regardless of the number of stitches needed.

This may seem somewhat difficult, but the worker will be surprised to find how easily it may be accomplished. It is optional with the worker as to the shape and size of the basket. One may have the flat, rose bowl or an absolutely straight-sided basket. After the worker has woven the desired size for the bottom, begin shaping, by placing the reed over the last woven coil according to shape desired. For instance, if an absolutely straight-sided basket is desired, place the reed *directly over* the last woven coil, and if a shallow basket, slightly raise the reed and continue to weave as before.

SHAPING THE BASKET.

This is for a *round* basket. The oval or canoe-shaped basket is shaped in a different manner. While it is more difficult to manipulate than the round basket, we are confident that if the worker will carefully follow our directions, they will not experience any difficulty whatever in giving that peculiarly beautiful swell to their basket which makes the Indian canoe basket such a pleasure to the collector.

Please observe that the *sides* of a canoe basket seem to be much *lower* than the *ends,* giving one the impression that extra coils have been introduced. This is not so, but this effect is gained by shaping the *ends only* at first.

Take an eight-inch length oval, start and after one has woven around five times, about one and one-half inches from each end, begin to shape by slightly raising the coil up onto the coil underneath. Continue weaving, (leaving the middle sides perfectly flat) until you have woven, say six rows, *before* you shape the *sides,* almost directly *over* the under coil. This gives that beautifully rounded appearance. The worker may have a long, narrow canoe, or a broader short one. This is controlled by the *width* of *bottom* of basket at the time when the shaping commences.

FINISHING.

To finish the edge of the basket, cut the reed to a small sloping point one and one-half inches long, and cover carefully. The last row of weaving will be stitching over and over the single reed. We would suggest that the last two rows be finished with colored raphia.

SPLICING THE REED.

To splice the reed, trim the ends to be spliced to flat points, placing together in such a manner that the uniform size of the reed may be kept. We advise beginners to fasten the reeds together with either a bit of wire or with dark thread. Take a small sewing needle, perforate the two ends of the reeds twice, draw wire or thread through and wrap around both firmly, cutting ends off. Should reeds prove unmanageable when released from the coiled package, and it is desirable to straighten them, holding a wet cloth in the hand, and pulling the reeds through the cloth a few times will be all that is necessary.

A Tulare Friendship Basket.

A friend, or tribe, desiring to show great respect or confidence toward another, presents as a mark of esteem a specially-woven basket, following about the same spiral lines of design. These lines, coming from the small basket bottom, represent the confidence and love which flows from their hearts to the recipient, the bottom of the basket representing the heart. This is a very handsome specimen of a friendship basket, its antiquity giving an indescribably beautiful coloring.

A Paiute Basket Showing Design of Flying Geese—Pomo Basket Showing Markings of an Animal—Yolo Basket With Quail Plumes and Diamond Shapes Representing Turtles.

Mono Cooking Basket.

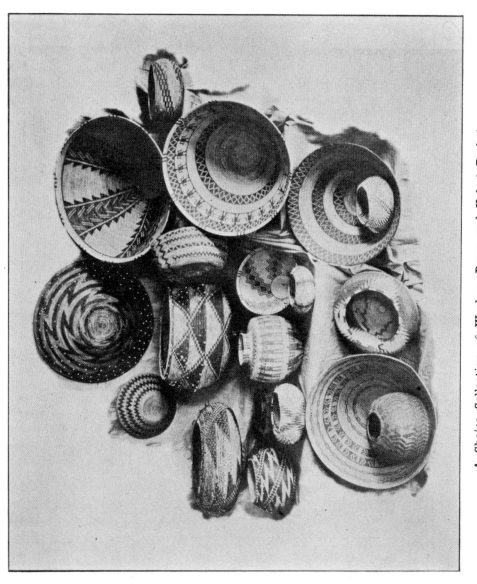

A Choice Collection of Washoe, Pomo and Yokut Baskets.

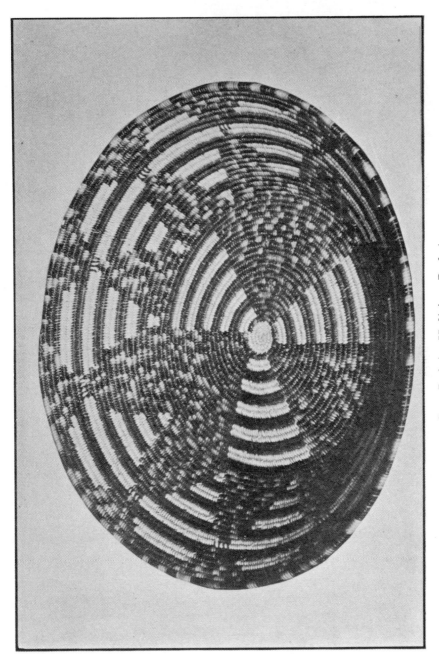

San Jacinto Medicine Basket.

CAHUILLA
COILED BASKET.

Showing Top and Sides of Basket.

The shape of
this basket is a
graceful one
with rounding
sides like a
rose bowl. The
design is effec-
tive and char-
acteristic.

Showing Bottom of Basket.

20

A WASHOE BASKET

Showing Top and Sides of Basket.

Design of conventionalized pine trees. The blocks in bottom of the basket represent low mountains with trees growing upon the sides.

Showing Bottom of Basket.

LAZY SQUAW WEAVE.

SHOWING COMMENCED BOTTOM, AND THE FINISHED BASKET.

SETTING UP THE BASKET.

To commence a round basket, proceed in the same manner as per our "general directions for a continuous-coil basket." By this, we mean preparing the reed, trimming of the reed, shaping into a coil, winding the raphia thread, and weaving until one coil of the reed is covered before beginning the "Lazy-squaw weave."

By examining the accompanying half-tone, you will see that it seems to be a *long* stitch and a *short* stitch, and it is here where an explanation of the name of the weave might be of interest.

If the squaw felt inclined to slight her weaving, she would wrap the single "bam" (reed) two, three or four times before taking the much harder long stitch which held the "bams" together, and so would receive from the other squaws harsh criticism, as well as the contemptuous appellation, "lazy squaw."

To return to our lesson; we now have our little coil ready for the long and

Lazy Squaw Basket.

short stitch. We gain this by holding the commenced coil in the left hand, and wrapping the raphia thread *toward* you and *around* the reed *once*. Then over the reed again and down through the center of the coil. This gives the *long* stitch, while wrapping the reed once, gives the *short* one.

Continue weaving in this manner one short stitch and one long stitch, coming toward you until ready for the design.

Weave on until the flat placque or bottom is five and one-half inches in diameter, then proceed with the design.

DESIGN.

A very simple and easy way in which to arrive at an exact division of the flat woven placque is to place it upon a piece of paper, mark around it with a pencil, cut out the outline and fold into the desired subdivisions. Replace upon the placque and mark upon it the divisions required for the design.

One can divide the sides in the same manner, being quite sure of the geometrical divisions, then mark the spaces either with a thread or pencil.

INTRODUCTION OF COLOR.

When the worker has decided upon the design and color to be used, we commence with the color, just as we weave with the natural raphia, splicing the thread in the same manner as we do in our "general directions" or first lesson.

Never cut off the different colors, but carry along *under* the weaving and *next* to the reed. Keep all colors threaded while being used in weaving, as it saves time.

SPLICING THE RAPHIA.

Follow our "general directions" given for a continuous coil basket, being careful to see that all ends are covered neatly and firmly, and please do not forget that the "lazy-squaw" weave comes *toward* the worker, not *from,* as in the Navajo weave.

SPLICING THE REED.

Follow the same directions given in our "general directions for a continuous coil basket."

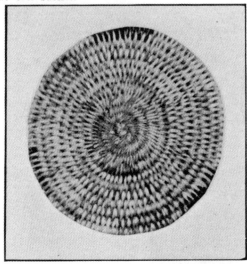

Commenced Basket, Lazy Squaw Weave.

FINISHING OFF THE EDGE OF BASKET.

One can follow the dictates of one's own judgment or use the directions given in our "general directions for a continuous coil basket." A solid row of color, or alternating blocks of color, make a desirable finish, as also the braided edge, which comes in a later chapter with the directions for weaving in shells and beads. The finished basket in the half tone which accompanies this lesson makes a very attractive waste-paper basket for the writing table or desk. It measures five and one-half inches across bottom, and stands six and one-half inches high, while the circumference of top, measures thirty-three inches. The colorings are very dainty. Materials used in its construction are as follows:

Number four reeds	5	ounces
Natural raphia	2½	ounces
Black raphia	¾	ounce
Orange	¾	ounce
Indian Red	I	ounce

Needles, number 18 blunt.

In weaving this basket, the raphia to be used is very coarse, but kept even. Many make the mistake of not keeping the fingers slightly moistened with water, while weaving. By so doing, the worker will find that the little fine fibers of the raphia will not wear up so readily and that the raphia seems to take on an almost polished surface, owing to some quality of the raphia which the moisture of the fingers seem to bring out.

YOLO BASKET.

Showing Top and Sides of Basket.

Bottom of Yolo Basket, Lightning Design.

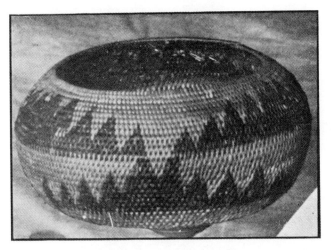

CACHE CREEK
TREASURE BASKET.

Showing Top and Sides of Basket.

Showing Bottom
of Cache Creek
Treasure Basket.

**TULE RIVER
TREASURE BASKET.**

Showing
Commenced Basket

Showing Top And Sides of Basket.

The design follows out the markings of a badger, and is woven in black and tan, with very small wampum decorations.

**Showing Bottom
of Basket.**

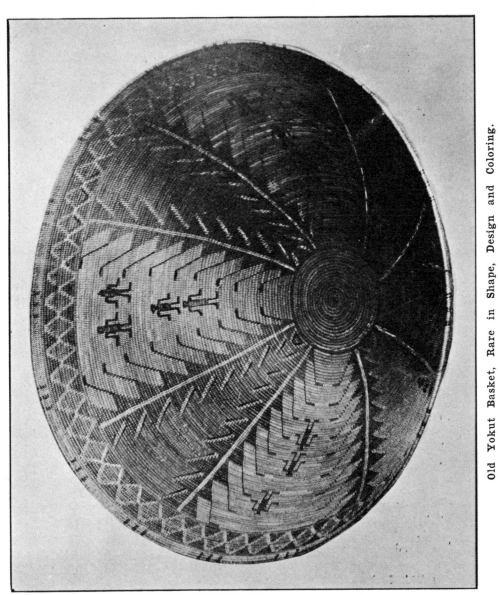

Old Yokut Basket, Rare in Shape, Design and Coloring.

MARIPOSA WEAVE.—(Knotted)

SHOWING COMMENCED BOTTOM OF BASKET, WITH FINISHED MARIPOSA BASKET.

The canoe-shaped basket, whose illustrations form a part of this lesson, has the very characteristic Indian design of butterflies. Anyone could add to its beauty by weaving in the white Indian beads in the dark-brown points. In a later chapter we shall give full directions for the weaving of beads.

SETTING UP THE BASKET.

In setting up the basket, you will observe that it is oval shaped. But the workers may follow out their own individual ideas as to the shape, etc., making the "start" longer or shorter as fancy dictates.

First—Cut the end of the reed off squarely. Measure off six, eight or ten inches (whatever is desired) upon the reed.

Commenced Basket, Mariposa Weave.

Take the reed in both hands and at the point marked off, bend it very slowly and carefully into a bowl of hot water, holding there fully five minutes.

Take the reed out and gently bend it, working with the fingers until you can bring the reeds together without breaking. Do not be dismayed should it split a little. It will do no harm, as it is covered with raphia. In our general directions for setting up an oval basket, we say soak the reeds *one* hour, in hot water, which is perhaps the better way until one has become more accustomed to handling the reeds. Some of our more experienced workers do not leave the reeds more than five minutes in very hot water, but they draw them through the fingers until they become quite pliable, and it really becomes optional with the workers in what manner they prepare the reeds after having had just about so much experience.

SELECTION OF RAPHIA.

Next thread your *large* needle with a *leaf* of raphia. Select uniform leaves, or place two strands together. Be careful to keep the thread the same size for the weaving. You will very soon see the necessity for so doing if you desire the beautiful results that the Indian women bring out in their weaving.

WEAVING.

Take the bent reed in your *left* hand, holding it so that the short end of the reed comes next you. Take your threaded raphia and about three or four inches from the end of the thread (not the needle end,) commence wrapping *toward* you (the *opposite* from the *Navajo weave,* which is wrapped *from* you,) two or three times around the bend of the reed. This is to cover the reed, and any little break or split that may have come in the shaping. When the bent end of the reed is covered smoothly, wrap once around the long reed, then over the long and short reed, binding them together.

Bring the needle up *between* the *two reeds* at the *left* side, and cross over this stitch which holds the two reeds together, going *down* between the reeds at the *right* side, and up, back of the crossed stitch, and coming over so as to wrap the *one* reed again, and then wrapping the two reeds as before.

This gives the knotted effect, by crossing the long stitch, holding the two reeds together, making a beautiful and substantial basket, capable of taking any design or shape.

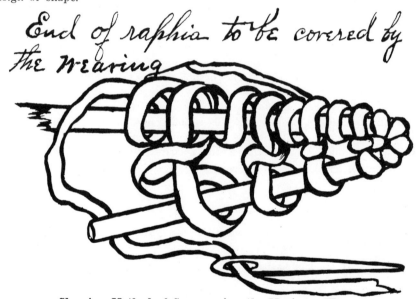

Showing Method of Commencing the Mariposa Weave.

THE INTRODUCTION OF COLOR.

The introduction of color for the design, may seem somewhat difficult, but we can assure the workers that they will be pleasantly surprised to find themselves weaving in the designs without any particular effort.

As we have said before, in our "general directions for a coiled basket," weaving in the color, means the filling in of a certain space, always, remembering that each coil is covered twice. It is this covering of the reed twice which may puzzle the worker, when putting in the design. Take your colored raphia and splice under the natural, just as we do in our "general directions" for a continuous-coiled basket, carrying the natural thread along under the colored, and reversing the order of things when weaving with the natural.

DIVISION FOR THE DESIGN.

Place your woven placque upon a piece of paper, mark around it and cut out the oval, folding it into such divisions as you desire your design to fill. Mark these clearly with a pencil, upon your placque, by placing the marked oval upon it.

We would suggest that the worker weave the bottom of the Mariposa basket two and one-half inches wide before beginning to shape the basket. However, it is optional as to the size, for if the bottom were broader, the sides would not be so high—just as the canoe whose shape has been copied. The beautiful shaping of these baskets by the Indians seems marvelous.

To give that swell peculiar to this shape, the worker will commence rounding the *ends only,* by placing the reed directly over the bottom reed already covered with weaving, leaving about seven and one-half inches upon each side flat, rounding up *only the ends* until the bottom is three and three-fourths inches wide. The basket is now ready for the shaping of sides. Do this by slightly raising the coil of reeds above the under coil, being careful to hold your reeds firmly while weaving.

While shaping, the thought might suggest itself to the worker, "Why, how am I to add in stitches to cover the added space of reed by the rounding out of the basket?"

This is very simple. Just add in where it seems best, an extra knotted stitch, which of course brings two in the space of one, but this does not show when the basket is finished. In the basket which we have used to illustrate this lesson, we have introduced the design at the same time that we commenced shaping the sides.

We give the measurements for this basket, and while the workers may use any design they desire, we selected this simple, but thoroughly Indian, idea of butterflies, thinking it would be less puzzling in the introduction of color than a more elaborate one. Use for this basket a coarse reed, No. 5.

Materials used in Mariposa basket:

Raphia, Natural .... 2½ oz.
Raphia, Brown .... 2 oz.
Reed, No. 5 .... 4½ oz.
Measurement of commenced "starter" .... 8½ in.
Measurement of width of bottom when shaping the ends .... 2½ in.
Width when ready for shaping sides .... 3¾ in.
Measurement of finished basket over outside *short* way........... 14 in.
Measurement of finished basket over outside *long* way.............23 in.

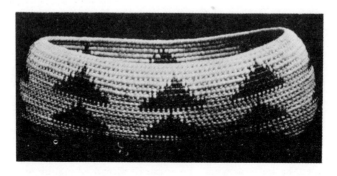

Finished Mariposa Basket.

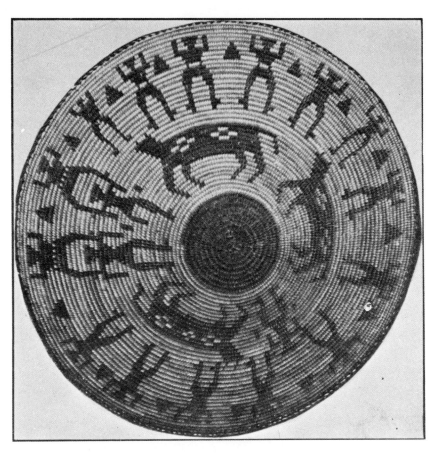

Apache War Basket, Very Shallow, Depth 4 inches, Circumference 51 3-4
Inches.   Design Black.

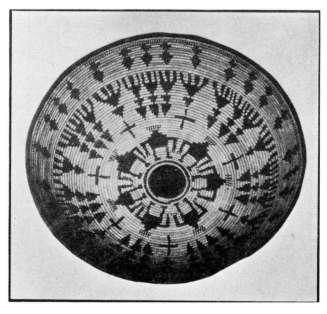

Apache War Basket.

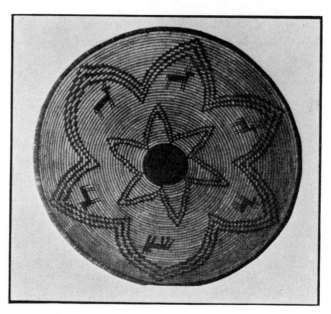

Apache Star Basket, Design Worked Out in Black.

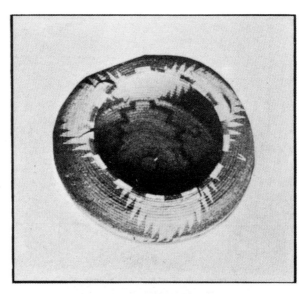

A Yolo Treasure Basket.

Baskets From San Jacinto Reservation.

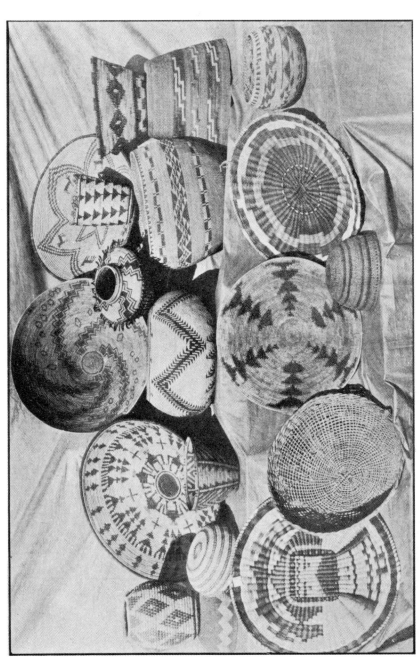

Coiled Hopi Tray.   Klamath Gambling Tray.   Klikitat Baskets.   Apache War Baskets and Pomo Upright Weaves.

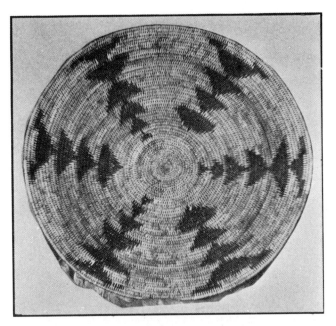

Klamath Gambling Tray, Showing Arrow Points.

A Saboba Ceremonial Basket.

TOAS WEAVE.

SHOWING THE BASKET COMMENCED AND FINISHED.

This weave gives a charming variety to a collection of baskets. The cut which accompanies this lesson shows the basket to be divided into eight sections. Four upright bands of weaving in knotted effect, and four plain spaces in which are placed the blocks with a man figure.

The "Toas Weave" is commenced as nearly all of the continuous-coil baskets are, under the directions given in our "General Directions for a Continuous Coil Basket." That is, in trimming the reed to a flat point, the wrapping of the reed with raphia and the weaving back over the thread until the reed is thoroughly covered.

When you have covered two coils of reed, carry your needle down through the center, coming up over the outer coil of reed and down again through the center. Do this eight times, thus giving the eight divisions—four for the plain and four for the knotted effect.

Showing Commenced Basket of Toas Weave.

TO WEAVE THE KNOTTED SECTIONS.

Bring the thread up over the top coil *toward* you, then wrap around the coil *once,* then over the two coils, coming up *between* the coils on the *left* side; now *cross* this stitch which holds the two coils together, going down upon the

36

right side of this stitch between the coils, coming up *behind* the single reed once and then again over the two reeds.

So continue weaving until this allotted space is filled, then up, over and down over the two reeds, which gives the dividing line between the plain and knotted sections.

TO WEAVE PLAIN SECTIONS.

In weaving this plain section, the stitch is taken just as if you were going to weave the plain Navajo weave, only wrap the reed *three* times and then take the Navajo stitch between the under coil. This is to give strength to the basket without showing that it is so strengthened. Please continue weaving until your flat placque is seven inches in diameter. However, this is optional with the worker, and the great charm of this work is the individuality which one seems compelled to bring out whether they so desire or not.

Should a larger or smaller basket be desired, this rests with the worker.

To introduce the color, first cut out of paper the shape of the blocks, and of the figure — spacing them evenly upon the basket after you have shaped and woven up five rows of weaving.

Looking at the cut of finished basket will help to make these instructions much clearer. The shaping commences by

Finished Lesson Basket, Toas Weave.

placing the top reed directly over the under reed and continuing the weaving, holding both reeds firmly.

The worker will please remember that in order to have a beautifully-shaped and evenly-woven basket, it is absolutely necessary to have both reed and raphia held *firmly,* the thread drawn in smoothly and reasonably tight. Practice alone gives confidence and confidence means one-half the battle.

For other directions, such as

Preparing the reed,	Introduction of color,
Threading the needle,	Shaping the basket,
To commence the basket.	Splicing the reed,
Splicing the thread,	Finishing,

consult our "general directions for continuous-coil basket."

The basket used as a model for this lesson measures five and three-fourths inches in height, diameter of bottom, seven inches and circumference of top, thirty-one and one-half inches.

We used black for the design, which was very effective with the natural raphia.

A MONO BASKET.

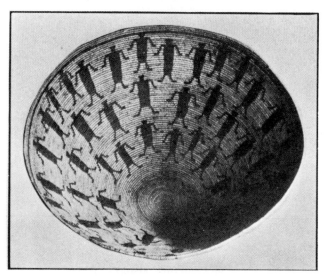

A POMO MAN BASKET.

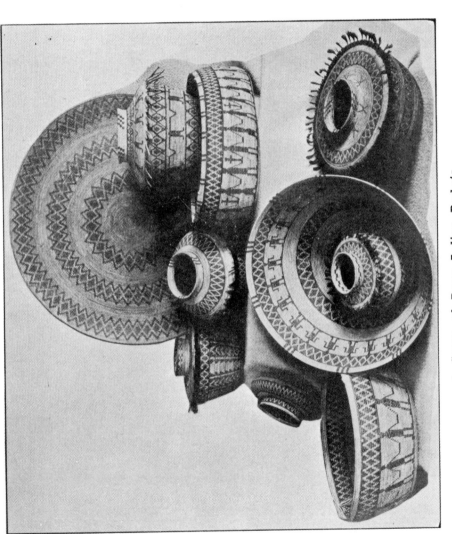

A Group of Pomo Indian Baskets.

The Pomos excel in the weaving, shaping and coloring of their Baskets. Some of their Treasure Baskets are so finely woven as to hold seventy or eighty stitches to the inch.

Cahuilla Meal Bowl.   Ute Winnower and Thompson River Baskets.

Apache and Pima Coiled Baskets.

SAMOAN WEAVE.— (Lace Effect)

SHOWING THE BASKET COMMENCED AND FINISHED.

The weaving of this dainty basket makes it especially suitable for the dressing table, or the numberless uses that ladies find for dainty boxes and baskets. Treasure baskets were the special pride of our dusky Indian maidens, and we feel confident that this basket will be much appreciated by our readers.

The half-tone of the commenced basket, as well as the finished one, will give some idea of the possibilities of this weave.

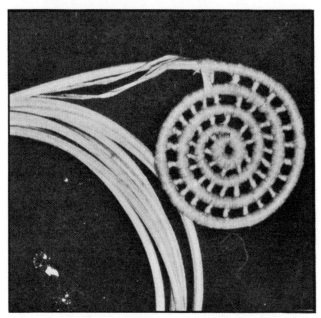

Commenced Basket of Samoan Weave.

A basket woven in No. 1 reed will make a fairy-like jewel case, and woven in No. 7 or 8 reed, with two full strands of raphia, will give a beautiful tray for cards, or make a charming fruit or nut basket.

For either tray or basket, make a flat placque, or mat, twelve or fourteen inches in diameter, with slightly-rounded sides, not having it more than one and one-half or two inches deep.

This weave gives splendid results for the time and labor expended upon it, being woven very quickly.

For this weave carefully read over our "general directions for a continuous coil basket." Commence this basket in exactly the same manner, and weave until you have covered four coils. Hold the *uncovered reed the distance from the woven coils that you desire for the lace part of your basket.*

Then wrap the thread *toward you,* around the single reed four times, going down between the coils with the fourth *wrapping stitch.*

We must caution the worker that right here comes the difficult part of this weave. This long stitch holding the two coils together must be held firmly, and the *open space between the reeds kept absolutely the same distance apart,* while you wrap around this raphia thread between the two coils, just as if you were taking two sewing stitches.

Then wrap the reed four times again, and so on until you have three rows of lace weaving. Then weave again the plain continuous coil for *four* rows, and so continue until the bottom of the basket is woven the desired size. Begin the shaping according to our "General Directions," putting any desired design into the plain band of Navajo weaving. The diamond or rattlesnake design would be very effective and thoroughly Indian.

The worker will not find it hard to follow the shape of the basket given to illustrate this lesson. The weaving of the top is really only a drawing in of the reeds. But they MUST be held *firmly* while they are woven.

Finished Lesson Basket, Samoan Weave.

This shaped basket is a very desirable one to have in a collection of baskets, and the Pomo bowls and bottle-necks are famous. This basket was modeled after a "chu-set" bowl. It stands three inches high, diameter of bottom where shaping commences, seven inches, circumference of largest part, thirty inches. Diameter of opening at top, five inches.

The secret of shaping these flat rounded baskets lies in having the flat placque large enough before the shaping begins.

Do not raise the first coil too abruptly. This must be done so carefully that it would be impossible to tell from the evenly-rounded sides where the shaping first began. Usually one becomes too impatient to see results, and if the work is hurried, the basket proves unsatisfactory. If the edge of this basket is finished off with a plain band of weaving, it will be quite as pretty as the lace band. It all depends upon the artistic sense of the worker.

> For other directions, such as
> Preparing the reed,
> Threading the needle,
> To commence the basket,
> Splicing the thread,
> Introduction of color,
> Splicing the reed,

consult our "general directions for a continuous-coil basket."

43

Yokut Treasure
Basket, With
Wampum and
Feather
Decoration.

Showing Bottom
of Yokut
Treasure Basket.

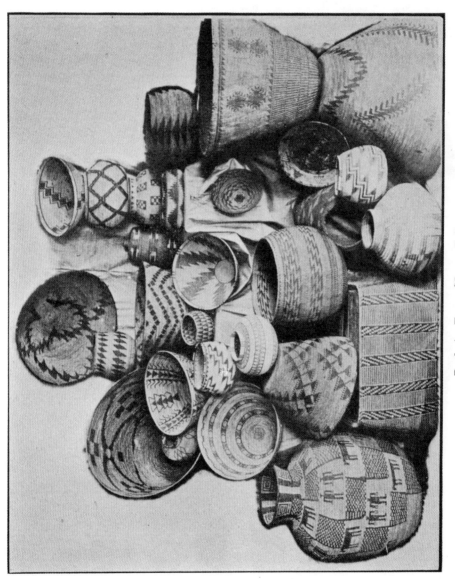

Baskets From Many Tribes.

Sacred Baskets of the Navajos, Apache, San Jacinto, and Pimas.

A Group of Aleutian Baskets.

KLIKITAT WEAVE.—(Imbricated)

We take great pleasure in giving this weave to our readers. It is capable of some beautiful results. In some localities, corn husks, (which dye beautifully) could be used for the over-lay; or wheat straws split, and soaked in water to make them pliable could be used; also the split palm leaves. All of these materials must be thoroughly dried after gathering. They would not take the dye satisfactorily otherwise.

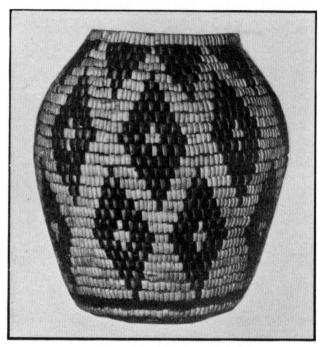

Finished Lesson Basket of Klikitat Weave.

These split straws give a beautiful surface in both the natural and dyed state, and have been used to some extent; but every worker who becomes interested in basketry, will find in every section of the country, that Nature has something to offer for the furtherance of this fascinating pastime.

The "Klikitat" baskets are becoming more rare, the squaws finding that civilization furnishes cooking vessels and carrying receptacles with much less expenditure of labor; and when we speak of labor we mean all that the word implies.

A genuine "Klikitat" basket represents days of hard work and often bruised, bleeding fingers. The *overlaying* weave being of the outer covering of bark or roots, which, when dried, are very harsh and unyielding. Some of these baskets are wonderfully beautiful, the overlaying taking on pearly opalescent tints which, contrasted with the deeper tones of rich browns in the designs, gives a mass of coloring which defies description.

These beautiful colorings are obtained in some instances by using various things. But the wonder of it all is, how does the Indian woman *capture* and *keep* these colors. We saw not long ago a splendid specimen of one of these baskets, over one hundred years old. It had seen much use, but was still firm and strong and exquisite in coloring. In some places the added stitch or "imbricated" weave had worn through the coil. Otherwise it was perfect.

We give this weave thinking it best for the worker to have the experience in setting up this shaped basket, which differs somewhat from the others.

The half tone which we depend upon to make clear the directions for this weave, is a genuine old "Klikitat" basket. Beautiful in coloring, and somewhat oval in shape, and a good design for a beginner, not being too elaborate. The body of the basket was tan colored (like the natural raphia) while the design was worked out in very dark brown, Indian blue and a dull yellow.

This basket stood seven and one-half inches high. Diameter of bottom (which was oval) through shortest part was three inches, and through longest, four and one-fourth inches. Circumference of largest part, twenty-two and three-fourths inches, and around the top, fourteen inches. While it is not necessary for the worker to follow this design, we would suggest that a small basket be woven first, putting in the "overlay" in straight bands of color.

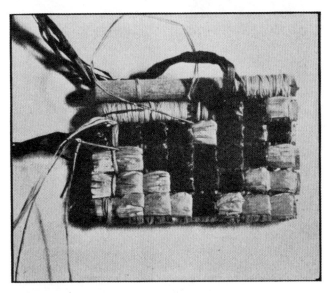

Showing Section of the Over-Lay Upon Klikitat Basket.

TO COMMENCE A BASKET.

Measure off *three* inches upon the end of reed. Soak the part of the reed to be bent, for about five minutes, by carefully bending into bowl of hot water. Take out of the water, wipe dry, and cut off end of reed squarely. Have needle threaded with a small thread of split raphia. Hold the reed in the left hand, with the short end next you, and the *bent* end pointing towards your *right* hand; the *ends* of reeds to your left.

Commence two or three inches from the end of the threaded raphia (not the needle end) and wrap *from* you around the bend of the reed, carrying the

49

short end of the thread along *under* the weaving until it has been covered for an inch. This is so that it may be securely fastened before cutting off the thread.

You work in the same manner, weaving the *two straight* reeds together, as for a "continuous" coil round basket. Each stitch or weave is passed between a stitch of the reed beneath, the passing of the thread *over* and *under* the *two* reeds form the figure eight, and is often called the figure eight stitch. This is the foundation for the "overlay imbricated" weave.

Weave until the bottom is of the desired size; shape the sides by placing the reed to be covered *directly over* the under reed, and so cover two coils up the side of basket with weaving for your "overlay."

Klikitat Basket, Showing Arrow Points in Design.

PREPARING THE OVER-LAY.

Take the material to be used for the overlay (raphia, straws or palm-fibres) and carefully fold it so as to make of it a flat ribbon. A leaf, or two leaves of raphia if needed, folded over twice (with outside edges stripped off to prevent drawing) and the edges folded inside will give a good, smooth, firm ribbon. For small reeds it will be necessary to split the raphia.

DESIGN.

Hold your basket firmly in the left hand. Have one end of your ribbon cut off squarely. Place this end onto your last coil, which has been *covered* by the weaving, being sure the cut ends point towards your left hand, and also that the right side of the ribbon shall come outside when it is folded over. Hold the ribbon in place while you weave *three* plain, straight "Navajo" stitches. These should cover the end of the ribbon firmly. Now fold the ribbon back over toward your *left* hand. The folding over of the ribbon covers the three stitches and end of ribbon. Take one stitch to hold the ribbon down in place. Again fold the ribbon toward your *right* hand, leaving enough folded to have the three stitches cover, and hold firmly the folded end of the ribbon. This time you take *four* stitches; the one extra stitch is taken *over,* and enough toward your *right* hand to *cover* the first stitch which held the ribbon while the folding was done. It is right here that exactness and care must be given not to show this stitch. The beauty of the "overlay" being spoiled if it shows the way in which the color is put on.

You continue now to weave *three* stitches, fold ribbon over, take one stitch; fold ribbon back toward right and take the one stitch right around and *over* the *one stitch* which held the ribbon, only taking it ahead and toward your *right* hand. This will cover every cross stitch, giving a beautiful effect, looking somewhat like pleating, but *firm* and *smooth*.

When you desire to change color, cut off the ribbon and place new color on in exactly the same manner as we gave directions for the first color.

To finish off the end of the ribbon cut surplus ribbon off, then carefully weave over it, covering the end very smoothly. We may have given the impression that the design only is put on in overlay, but this is not so; as often the bottom has been woven in the plain Navajo weave, the rest of the basket being finished in the imbricated.

For other directions such as

Preparing the reed,
Threading of the needle,
To commence the basket,
Splicing of the thread,
Introduction of color,
Design,
Shaping the basket,
Splicing the reed,

Please follow the general directions.

The finish of this basket around the top could be plain or like the ornamental top of the second basket.

Showing Top of Basket.

Rather low, flat and bowl shaped. Different from treasure baskets of other tribes. The design runs zigzag from the bottom, curving in a spiral manner to the top. The opening is very small. The sides are bulging and well rounded.

Showing Bottom of Mariposa Treasure Basket.

Three Choice Bottle-Neck Baskets. Little Men, Pomo. Upright Design, Mono. Snake Design, Yokut.

SHI-LO BASKET.—(Two Bam)

SHOWING COMMENCED BASKET AND ILLUSTRATING THE MANNER IN WHICH TO PREPARE THE SHELLS AND BEADS FOR WEAVING.

This is a beautifully shaped canoe basket, ornamented with shells and beads, and we can assure the worker that this basket with its corrugated surface and delicately rounded sides, will more than repay the expense and time given to its weaving.

The shades of raphia in dull Indian red, bright cardinal and natural raphia with the white Indian beads, and delicately tinted shells, make a very attractive color scheme. The Indians only use this weave in their more elaborate gift or ceremonial baskets. Hence it follows that they are not very often found in the curio stores. The name " Shi-lo " means two reeds, or that two bams are used in its construction, and it is the use of the very large reed and a fine one which gives the beautifully corrugated appearance. We give an outline drawing of bottom of this basket, showing the divisions for color, as well as the sides of basket, to illustrate the following directions:

Shi-lo Basket.

TO COMMENCE THE BASKET.

The " Shi-lo " is commenced in exactly the same manner as an oval Navajo weave, and so woven for the first center length of reed, and one row of weaving around that. The worker will measure off eleven inches from one end of reed (having the other coiled into a convenient coil and tied firmly.) Soak the reed at point marked, by carefully bending into a bowl of boiling water and holding it there about five minutes; take the reed out and pull between the fingers to make pliable. Now bend at point marked, very slowly and carefully, bringing the two reeds together. Should they split a little do not be dismayed—the raphia will cover all defects. Have your needle ready, threaded with natural raphia. Now with the left hand take the bent reed, holding it firmly, with the short end next you and both ends pointing toward your left hand. Commence weaving just as you do in the plain Navajo weave,

54

being careful to smoothly cover the bent part of the reed. Continue weaving until you have a center rib, or reed, and one row around covered with the plain weaving, which means the covering of three reeds.

INTRODUCTION OF LITTLE REED.

By examining the half tone which shows the weaving, the worker will see that the small reed comes between, and divides the large reeds. Also that the small reed is covered only *once,* while the large reed is covered twice with the weaving. We are now ready to insert the new reed,—which has been trimmed to a point,—by placing the small reed between the large reeds, just after the curve has been made, being sure that the sharpened point of the reed is pushed up closely to the upper reed under the last woven stitch. Now commence weaving *toward* you, the very opposite of the Navajo weave. Then *down under* the *small reed* and *up between* the small and large reed, *over* the larger reed, which is the under reed, up again between the small and large reed and *over* the small reed, down between the small and large reed, coming up again *over* the top reed *toward* you. You are again ready to repeat the process.

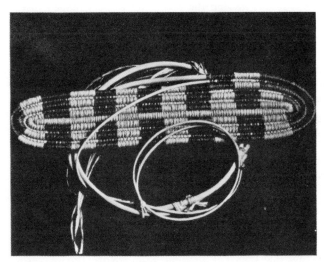

Bottom of Shi-lo Basket, Showing The Little Reed in
Place.

You will observe that the small reed is only covered *once* while the large reed is covered twice.

SHAPING THE BASKET.

We cannot impress upon the worker too strongly the importance of carefully shaping the basket. In the first place the reeds must be held *firmly* and the weaving drawn reasonably tight, also all ends of the raphia threads covered neatly and smoothly.

The secret of shaping a canoe lies in its being commenced rightly. If the first curving upward of the reed has been too abrupt, no after attempt to pull it into shape will avail.

To shape the canoe whose dimensions are given with this lesson, commence with the *sixth* row of weaving (counting from the center row out, and including both coarse and fine reeds as one.) To give the swell peculiar to this shaped basket, begin by raising the upper reeds above the lower ones, at *each end* of the flat bottom, leaving the sides to be woven flat for nine and one-half inches on each side. Continue raising the ends and keeping the sides flat until you have woven four or five rows more, then shape your sides by placing the upper reeds almost directly over the lower row of weaving; continuing of course to swell the reeds out and upward until the largest desired dimension has been reached.

To shape the top in smaller is easier than giving the swell, and only means to draw the reeds in, holding them firmly while doing so.

TO WEAVE IN THE BEADS.

The Indians do not use colored beads upon their baskets, as a rule, but the small white beads of a somewhat irregular shape are strung upon a strong cord. We use a coarse grey carpet thread of linen which answers our purpose admirably. String your beads upon this thread, securing the one end so that the beads may not lose off, leaving the other end to be wrapped three times around the large reed. Cover both the wrapping and end of thread by weaving an inch or more; this is so that the end may be securely fastened. Now slip a bead up close to the last stitch of raphia, not leaving the linen thread too loose, and still not drawing it too tight, which would cause it to wear unnecessarily. Continue weaving as before, always carrying the thread along next to the reed. The beads may be dotted irregularly over the portion of the design to be ornamented, or a set number used, making a geometrical design. However, this rests with the individual taste of the worker, for the Indian baskets are decorated after both styles.

The beads are generally placed upon a dark colored portion of the design, which certainly adds to the effectiveness of the whole.

WEAVING IN THE SHELLS.

Select the number of shells to be used for the finish, cut the same number of six-inch lengths from your linen thread. Knot one end of each of these threads, making the knots large and firm. Now thread through the shell, drawing the knot up firmly into the shell. If this is carefully done your shell cannot slip off, although one could use a small seed bead instead of knotting the thread. After the shell is threaded with the linen thread, string on three beads. It is now ready to weave in. Wrap the thread *three* times around the large reed, being careful to cover with the weaving. Do not draw up too close to the reed, but leave it to swing loosely. Do not cut off the end of your thread until you are ready to weave in another shell; and it would really be better to carry the old thread along and wrap the new thread over it. However, the worker's own good judgment will guide as to the better way.

TO FINISH THE BASKET.

The worker may finish in any one of the several ways, using one color, or weaving in alternate blocks of color. But to have a good, strong substantial edge, cut off the small reed and place the large reed directly over the lower reed, and *enclose both* reeds with the *one* stitch, covering thickly and smoothly with the weaving. The basket used as a model had alternate blocks of color worked over the two reeds. The shells are always woven in one reed, *below* the last row woven for the finish. We mean by this that the shells must not be woven in on the finishing row of weaving.

Read our general directions for "A Continuous Coil Basket," for the splicing of the larger reed.

To splice the small reed, cut end off squarely and place the new reed over the old one, one inch and continue weaving in both reeds. One might think this not a very substantial way to splice, but it holds firmly, only one must be careful to see that the new reed is not handled carelessly until it has been woven in three or four inches; otherwise it might be easily pulled out, but once secured it is firm and strong.

For introduction of color and threading needles, we again ask you to be kind enough to re-read our "Continuous Coil Directions."

For this basket we used a number

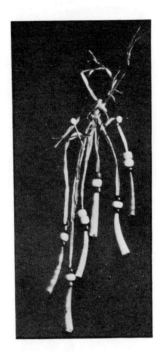

Showing Method of Stringing the Beads and Shells for Weaving Shi-lo Baskets.

six reed for the large reed, and number one for the small one. However, the size of the reeds is immaterial, the one idea being to have the two reeds very different in size, and if one desired, a much finer reed could be used for the large one and a number " oo " for the small one.

To commence this basket measure off the reed 11 in. Width of the bottom when ready for the design for the sides, 3½ inches.

Width of basket inside, 4¾ inches.

Measurement over the outside the short way, giving the swell which is not so great as at the ends, 14½ inches.

Measurement over the swell, long way, 27 inches.

Reeds, No. 6 (large) .... 6½ oz.
Reeds (fine) .... 1¼ oz.
Needles (tapestry) ....No. 20.
Raphia (natural) .... 6 oz.
Indian Red .... 3 oz.
Cardinal Red (bright) .... 1 oz.
White Indian beads .... 2 oz.
Horn Shells .... ½ oz.
Linen Thread .... 1 skein.

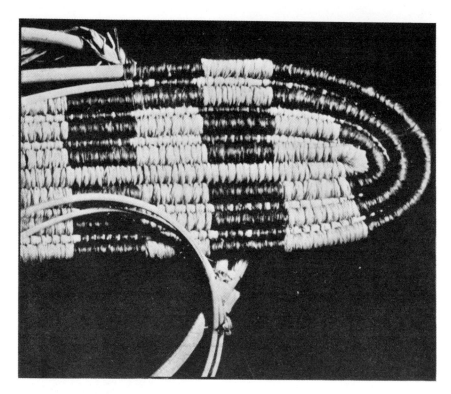

Showing Magnified Section of Shi-lo Weave.

A Santa Ysabel Basket.

A Collection of Baskets, Navajo School of Indian Basketry.

BAM-TSU-WU BASKET.—(Three Bam)

SHOWING COMMENCED BOTTOM ALSO TOP AND SIDES OF FINISHED BASKET.

This weave, while very decorative, we do not consider as practical and durable as many of the more closely woven weaves. However, some beautiful results can be obtained by staining the reeds in different colors before weaving, and using the natural or some harmonizing shade of raphia for the weaving.

The worker must insist upon having the best quality of polished reeds for this basket, owing to the open spaces between the rows of spiral weaving, which leaves the reeds uncovered.

One can readily see the artistic possibilities in having the reed stained and also the absolute necessity for using *good* reeds.

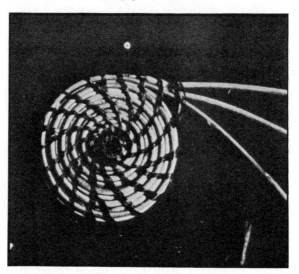

Commenced Basket, Using Three Reeds or Bams.

TO COMMENCE YOUR BASKET.

Select *three long* reeds, coil all separately into neat coils (firmly tying) leaving about three feet uncoiled. Soak ten inches of the uncoiled ends in boiling hot water for two hours. At the end of that time remove from the water, wipe dry with a cloth, and very carefully prepare them for the coiling by making them pliable, which means to gently pull them through the fingers, shaping them into coils. When sufficiently soft and pliable, trim each reed to a flat point about two inches long. Now place all of the reeds together with the *flat* points laying one on top of the other; fasten these firmly together with a *fine* dark-colored *thread,* sewing the flat points together for an inch or more. This will be covered by the weaving of raphia so that the thread stitches cannot possibly show. Have a rather large sized tapestry needle threaded with a coarse thread of the desired shade of raphia. Take your reeds into your left hand, wrapping the end of the raphia thread around one reed once or more, which helps to hold it. Then wrap firmly around the flat point. Be very careful at

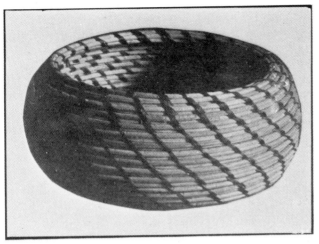

this part of the work not to split or break your point while forming the coil, which must be as small as possible and perfectly round.

After the coil is properly formed, secure it by sewing down through the center, and coming up, and over, all of the three reeds, continuing until the coil is firmly covered with the weaving. It is somewhat difficult to hold the

Showing Top and Sides of Three-Reed Basket, Bam-tsu-wu.

three reeds at once, and give good firm weaving, but it can be done. Great care must be given that the reeds are each kept to its proper place, or we lose the corrugated effect which really is the charm and novelty of this basket.

To hold the reeds properly means the *two* reeds lay close side by side, while the *third reed* lays on top, or as the basket is woven, this top reed comes in *between* the two reeds which lie side by side (flat), giving the corrugated appearance so much desired.

We use only one color for the weaving, and by closely examining the accompanying illustration, you will see that the weaving runs around necessitating the adding in of a new row of weaving at regular intervals. However, this will largely depend upon the shape you desire for your basket, as for example a large, flat bottomed basket would require more of the added in rows of weaving than a rose bowl shaped basket.

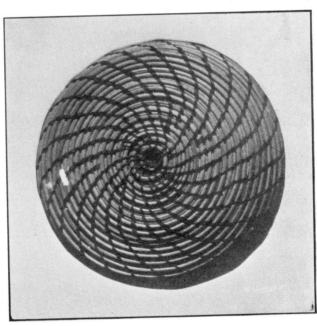

Showing Bottom of Three-Reed Basket, Bam-tsu-wu.

TO SPLICE THE REED.

Trim the ends of both new, and old reeds to be spliced, to flat points so that when fitted together they shall form a perfectly rounded reed of the required uniform size. Fasten these ends of reeds together with a number fifty thread (dark shade) by taking two or three stitches and tying the ends together. Do not knot the thread. If the worker is using the stained reeds, please cover the splicing with raphia of the same shade as the reeds, taking great care to have the raphia ends tied together smoothly so they are sure to come upon the *inside*. This may seem not a neat and substantial manner of treating the reeds, but it really is quite strong and durable. The splicings should always come in different places, no two coming together; and there being *three* reeds, the strain does not come upon them singly.

TO SPLICE THE WEAVING THREAD.

This is very simple. Always leave a sufficiently long end of the weaving thread to enable the worker to tie on a new thread, drawing it firmly and closely to the *inside* of the basket, being careful not to cut the ends too short. If it were possible, a more substantial method for splicing both reed and raphia should be given, but the weaving being so very open, prevents any other way of doing.

SHAPING THE BASKET.

To shape the basket, please follow the General Directions given for all continuous coil baskets, considering the *three* coils as *one* reed. By slightly raising the coils of weaving above each other, will give a rounded bowl shape, or for a straight-sided basket, place the coils of weaving directly *over* each other. Shaping the basket is largely individual, and is really giving expression to individual ideas of what one considers artistic and symmetrical in shape. The Indian women rarely ever weave two baskets alike in shape and design.

FINISHING THE TOP.

When the basket has been woven the required size, finish by weaving a double row ot *two* "bams" or reeds around the top, cutting out the one reed, or the middle reed. If this reed has been trimmed to a flat point, it will hardly show where it ended.

Carefully lay your *two* reeds around the top *inside* the basket, endeavoring to keep the weaving stitches, which holds the two reeds in place, exactly *over* each preceding stitch that held the *three* reeds. This is so that the basket may not show that the two coils are added inside to strengthen the top, and that the effect of the spirals of weaving may not be lost. When the last coils have been woven, trim the ends of the two reeds to flat points, covering them firmly with the weaving, and tying the raphia thread upon the inside of the basket as the final finishing touch. The reader will please refer to our directions given for staining the reeds, which will be given with the directions for dyeing the raphia in the last part of this book.

Washoe Basket of Magnificent Proportions, Showing Design of Tree, Measures 69 1-2 Inches in Circumference. Diameter of Bottom 7 inches, Height 15 Inches.

Skokomish Baskets, Characteristic in Shape and Design.

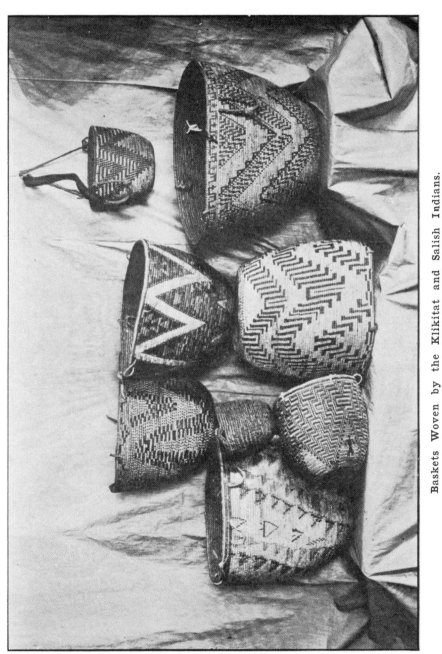

Baskets Woven by the Klikitat and Salish Indians.

BASKET FINISH.

This beautiful finish, somewhat resembling a braided whip handle, is a distinguishing finish of the Navajo and Paiute Indians, although we find many Apache baskets finished in the same manner. However, collectors have proven beyond a doubt that this weave originated with the Navajo weavers.

This substantial and really beautiful finish is given the basket after the last row of weaving has been completed. That is, the reed has been cut off, and trimmed down to a flat point, and covered with weaving, the weaving thread being fastened in securely, and cut off.

Basket Finish Showing Braided Effect.

The basket is now ready for the braided effect or finish. Take a large needle (No. 18), thread with a full leaf of medium sized raphia, natural or the darker shade, used in weaving the basket design. Take threaded needle in the *right* hand, and commence weaving by sewing *under* the *last* coil, and coming toward the worker. To illustrate the point, if for instance, the finished basket is placed upon a table, commence weaving upon the right hand side. The needle being pushed through *between* the two top coils, from the *outside,* or right hand side of the basket, and coming out upon the *inside* of the basket. Now come up *over* the coil, or reed, and forward, just in advance of the starting point, sewing backward and forward as one would coil a kite string. With a little practice the worker should be able to give a smooth braided effect to the edge of the basket. If one desired, a larger reed might be woven in for the finish, and the braided effect woven over it. Many of the grain placques of the Apaches are so finished, giving added strength as well as beauty to the finish.

WEAVING OF SHELLS, BEADS AND FEATHERS.

The Pomo Indians excel in this mode of beautifying their baskets, and some exquisite specimens of Indian weaving are marvels of coloring.

Rare feathers, rivaling jewels in their brilliancy; Abalone shells which when cut and polished seem like imprisoned sunsets, these together with the soft pearl white of the wampum give a color scheme which would satisfy the soul of a Raphael.

While it would be impossible to reproduce these Indian works of art, we can give some of their methods whereby the worker may, with the material at hand, gain some splendid results.

All cannot possess these gems of Indian art, and yet much pleasure and appreciation may be given to all lovers of basketry by more fully understanding and studying the work of these people. While we are not able to use some of their materials, and lack the dexterity of their fingers, yet it is possible to bring out some good results.

A Feathered Ceremonial Yokut Basket.

The Indians have very appropriately named this basket the "Feathered Jewel." One cannot possibly do justice in attempting to describe the iridescent coloring of pink and green in the cut abalone shells — the dainty pearl white of wampum decoration against a background of exquisite blues, greens and yellows of natural feathers, which gives a color scheme that rivals the rain-bow tints. This basket measures 17 inches in length by 6¼ inches in width.

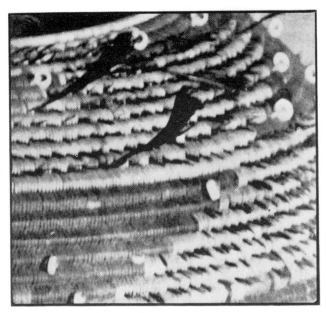

Enlarged Section of Pomo Shi-pus Basket Showing Method of Beading.

A Thompson River Basket, Good in Shape and Design.

68

WEAVING OF SHELLS.

The Indians cut bits of Abalone shells into pendants of different shapes; but they generally follow some geometric form. The cutting and polishing of these shells represent weeks of hard work, but the results justify the means, and we can assure our readers that by sending to any of the several firms on this coast who cut and polish shells for the general market, they can get exact duplicates of the Abalone shells used by the Indians. The dealers will cut them to order in any size or shape, singly or by the dozen or quantity.

The worker will feel more than repaid by the addition of these dainty bits of coloring to their weaving.

The Horn shells can also be bought from dealers in shell goods by the package or by the pound.

To weave the Abalone shells, cut into six-inch lengths as many lengths of strong grey linen carpet thread as there are Abalone pendants to be woven. String onto each of these lengths of thread eight beads (medium sized), two white and

Choice Pomo Feathered Basket With Beads and Cut Abalone Shell Decoration.

two red, alternating, until the eight beads are used up. Now string on the shell, passing the thread back up through the beads. It is now ready to weave into the basket. Wrap the thread around the reed *three* times. Do not pull the pendant up too close to the reed, but leave it to swing easily. Keep the forefinger of the left hand upon the end of the thread, until the *three* wraps have been securely covered by the raphia weaving; do not cut off the end of the thread, but carry it along next the reed, and let it be covered with weaving. After a little practice the worker will find no difficulty whatever in covering over the pendant threads with the raphia.

TO WEAVE THE HORN SHELLS.

The worker may cut off as many six-inch lengths of grey linen carpet thread (or raphia thread is very artistic) as the number of shells to be woven. These may be placed one-half inch apart, or as best pleases the worker. Knot each end of the six-inch lengths of threads with a large firm knot, and firmly draw these knotted ends *up into* the horn shell. This will keep the shell in place. Next thread on the large or medium size beads of different shades (say three beads, two white and one pink or green.) After the required number of the strung shells and beads are ready, proceed exactly in the same manner as one weaves in the Abalone shells.

A Pomo Ceremonial Basket. Magnificent in Shape and Coloring. These are Often Called, and Very Appropriately so, "A Feathered Jewel." A Pomo E-pi-ca.

A Magnificent Pomo Shi-pus Basket.

(This basket is an unusually good specimen of fine weaving and shaping.)

THE WEAVING OF FEATHERS.

In the weaving of beads, the Indians follow a geometrical design quite as often as dotting or scattering them irregularly over some portion of a solid color in the design. The worker will see this illustrated in some of the beautiful baskets which we have had reproduced for this book. The Indians when weaving in the beads or wampum use a very strong dark colored hemp thread of their own manufacture, and for the beading alone, string a great many upon a long thread, and then wrap this beaded thread around a piece of bark to keep the thread from being tangled.

Our white workers would prepare the beads in the same manner, and commence weaving by wrapping one end of the thread around the reed three times, close to the last stitch of raphia weaving. Hold the end of the thread firmly by pressing it against the reed with the forefinger of the left hand while covering the wrapped hemp thread with the raphia weaving. With a little practice the worker will find no difficulty in covering this thread. Do not cut off the end of bead thread, but carry it along next to the reed, and cover it with the weaving.

The thread being firmly fastened, slip a bead up close to the last stitch of raphia weaving; do not draw the bead thread too closely or too tightly, but leave the bead somewhat loose, so that it may not wear the thread. Carry the thread along next the reed until ready for another bead; do not cut it off, but leave it a long, continuous thread with the beads woven in irregularly or following some geometrical pattern.

When at the end of the thread, finish it off securely by wrapping it around the reed two or three times, and either commence a new thread, wrapping over the old bead thread, or finish by covering with the raphia weaving.

A word in regard to the colored beads. The Indians, as a general thing, use a creamy white bead when beading their baskets, showing their good judgment by so doing, as the colored beads, unless very carefully selected, would certainly mar the general effect. The use of the gaily-colored beads takes precedence in the ornamentation of their belts, tobacco pouches, necklets and other trappings.

The Indians secure the brilliant colored feathers from the different birds. for their weaving. They never dye the feathers used for this purpose. However, should the worker be fortunate enough to possess some bright colored birds' plumage, such as the breasts, bodies or wings, as well as the effective black or peacock's feathers, they could very successfully weave a Pomo "Shipus " for themselves.

The feathers are laid on next to the reed, the stem end pointing to the *left hand.* This is covered with the weaving and the feathers are laid on at regular intervals and overlap each other. Care must be taken to draw the raphia weaving thread tight. The Indian squaw weaves in so firmly that one *cannot* pull the feathers out,—they break off instead.

We give the following description of a small feathered basket, which belongs to a choice collection of Indian baskets, and will show that of a necessity these feathered treasures are rare and almost priceless. It took to weave this basket, the feathers from the heads and throats of one hundred and nineteen small duck, nearly as many wook-peckers, a number of wild canaries (for the yellow feathers) and eighty quail for the quail plumes.

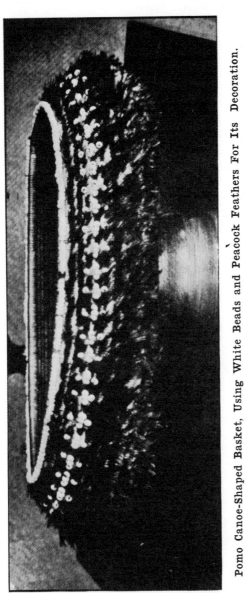

In this collection was also a peacock feathered basket, which was a beautiful mass of coloring. We would suggest the weaving of a small canoe-shaped feathered jewel tray, quite flat, and not more than one and one-half inches deep. Use a No. 1 reed with cut Abalone pendants and peacock feathers. To use the peacock feathers, trim out the center rib of the feather, which will leave a fringe upon each side. Divide this fringe into small bits and weave them in as one would weave a single feather, overlapping enough so that one could not distinguish where the feathers had been woven in.

For a border use white beads with small cut Abalone shells for the pendants, and a closely woven row of beads around the top.

Use two threads of strung beads, keeping each thread separate. Slip up two beads at a time, weaving as for a single bead.

Have Abalone shells cut the size of a small wampum, that is, about one-half inch in diameter with a fairly good-sized hole in the center, which allows the heavy thread to hold them flat. These are held in place by two stitches and gives a beautiful edge finish. Nearly all of the jewel or feathered baskets are so finished.

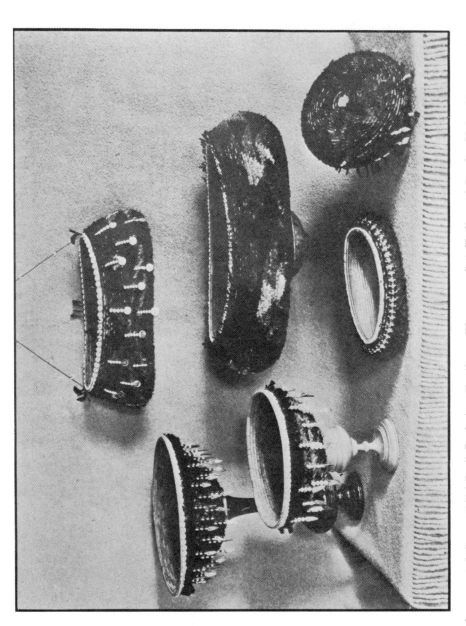

Ornamented Pomo "Shi-Bu" Basket.   Feathers, Wampum, Cut Shells and Beads, Make These Baskets
Indian Gems of Art.

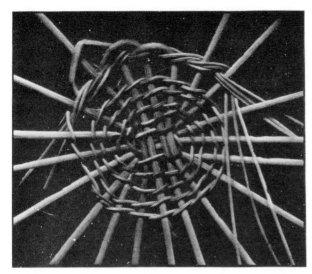

Showing Commenced Winnowing Tray, Also Manner of Finishing Edge. For This Basket use 5 ounces each, of Nos. 1 and 3, of polished rattan.

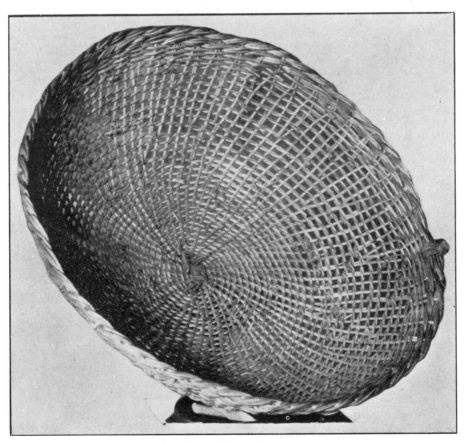

Dieguino Winnowing Tray.

POMO BAM-TUSH BASKET

THIS LESSON BASKET FULLY ILLUSTRATED, SHOWING EACH STEP IN ITS CONSTRUCTION

The weaving of a fine Pomo "bam-tush" is the poetry of Indian weaving, and this method of construction lends itself to the most delicate and beautiful twined work of the Pomo Indians.

The "Chu-set" of which we shall speak later is very similar in appearance to the "bam-tush," although it is not so strong and durable, but is considered the most beautiful of the Pomo weaves. However, it is the "bam-tush" basket which fills the every day needs.

Strong, well-woven baskets, capable of holding water, as well as being used for cooking vessels, grain placques, storage baskets, mortar baskets, burden baskets, and mush-bowls, are oftenest found in this weave, and while being put to such homely every-day uses, they are many times ornamented with most beautiful designs.

What housewife among the Indian woman's white sisters would so ornament the utensils for every day use, combining beauty of form as well as color in the most common household belongings,— not many we fancy.

But to return to our lesson. The Indians use bams made from the willow, or some other equally tough, pliable material, which have been carefully prepared in uniform sizes. But the white workers have been saved all of this necessarily hard labor of preparing their reeds, for we are able to turn to the different sized rattans and gain practically the same results with very much less work. These reeds or rattans can be bought in small quantities at any large basket factory, or where the willow or rattan furniture is sold.

Select a *good* quality of No. 1 reed, and should the worker desire to have an exact reproduction of some of the Indian baskets,— by using *flat* reeds (bams) instead of round ones,— run the reeds through a clothes wringer, which will flatten them without splitting, if not too much pressure is used. We have used very successfully an old photographic burnisher for this purpose.

After the worker has decided,— flat "bams" or round ones,— we will then commence our basket, supposing, of course, that all of the needed materials are at hand, which consists of the following:

2 oz. No. 1 reed (polished).
¼ oz. bright red raphia.
¼ oz. Irish green raphia.
¼ oz. Indian blue raphia.
¼ oz. orange yellow raphia.
1 oz. natural raphia.

The probable cost of your raphia would be about 15c; the cost of your reeds 25c. This will give a basket of upright weave about five inches tall and eighteen inches in circumference.

TO COMMENCE BASKET.

Cut eight lengths of fifteen inches each from your round or flattened reeds. Take four "bams" laying them parallel to each other, and one thread of raphia natural. Take an ordinary leaf of raphia and split into three threads and weave over and under through the center of the bams until you have a square of weaving, taking the width of your "bams" for the measurement as in Fig. 1 of the illustration. Make two of these sets of weaving, keeping your work flat upon a table or smooth board. Now place these *two sets* of woven "bams" together, crossing them at right angles, and having the two long ends of the raphia threads meeting as in Fig. 2 of the illustration. Have these threads placed so that they will weave *toward* your *right*. Next take the two threads of raphia, one in each hand, select the "bam" nearest and commence your weaving by crossing the threads. (Some give an extra cross or twist before taking the next "bam.") So continue weaving until you have bound the eight "bams" together. Upon the second row around, add in two extra "bams" in the corners where the sets of weaving cross each other. After several rows of weaving begin spreading the first eight "bams" making all diverge from a common center. The idea now is to have a flat, smoothly woven placque with evenly distributed "bams." No. 3 of the illustration will show the manner in which the "bams" are put in at the corners, and wherever needed to give a uniform divergence.

The "bams" to be inserted are always sharpened, that is, the round

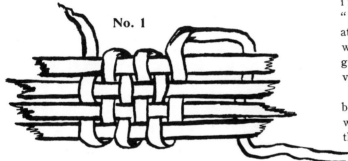

No. 1

ones are carefully trimmed to points, while the flat ones are cut to a point with a pair of scissors.

The new "bams" are pushed down beside an old "bam"—a piece of sharpened wire or stiletto would open the meshes of weaving enough to allow the point of "bam" to go in. The squaw uses a bone awl made usually from the thigh bone of some fowl or animal.

SPLICING THE THREAD.

Keep all of your threads the same width. This is absolutely necessary for smooth, uniform weaving. First cut off one end (the hard end) of the raphia thread; let one and one-half inches of the thread remain on the inside of the basket, while you weave

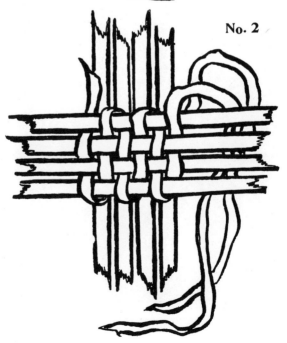

No. 2

the *new* thread along with the *old* thread until you have woven about one and one-half inches. Then push the old thread to the inside of the basket which means the under side as it lays flat upon the table. After you have woven around and past your old end of thread about an inch, you can then cut off the ends of both old and new threads if they interfere very much with your weaving. Should the points or ends of your "bams" slip through, or if it would be easier to *lay* them in instead of making an opening for the new "bam" at the side of the old "bam" (both methods are used), which, of course, would leave ends upon the inside of the basket. Do not trim off the ends of these "bams" until your basket is almost finished.

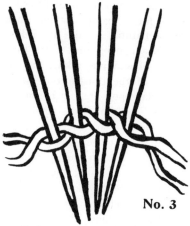

No. 3

The Indian women do not trim their baskets until they are completed. But we advise trimming the ends as seems most convenient to the worker.

INTRODUCTION OF COLOR.

To weave in the color, select the desired shades, keeping it the same width as the natural raphia thread. Drop one natural raphia thread, pushing it back under your weaving; place your thread of color in its place, leaving a one and one-half inch end to be slipped under the placque too. Continue weaving and the worker can readily see that it brings out a band, with stitches of alternating color.

SOLID BAND OF COLOR.

Take two threads of any desired shade, twist them firmly together one and one-half inches from the end. It is not good weaving to tie knots. Place these twisted ends under the placque, where the former weaving threads have

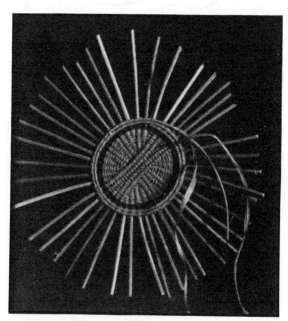

Commenced Bottom of A Pomo Bam-tush.

been pushed out of the way. Carefully p u s h the new threads close to the old threads, not allowing any break in the weaving owing to the skipping of a "bam."

Take a thread of color in each hand, and continue weaving as before, being careful to push each row of weaving up to the preceding row and see that each "bam" is held firmly in place. When changing color always firmly twist the threads together before leaving them under the placque. The basket cut which accompanies this lesson is very simple and dainty in design, and yet illustrates the introduction of color in a manner that cannot puzzle the beginner as some of the more elaborate baskets of the same weave, which may be found in the collections of half tones which accompany the lessons.

SHAPING THE BASKET.

The Indian woman when weaving finds a small sized tree trunk of a convenient height to fit her needs, which means a small flat surface about three feet from the ground. She places the basket, which is ready for shaping, (that is, she has woven the flat placque to the required size) upon the top of this smooth surface tree trunk, holding the flat placque firmly in place by weighting it with a rock or stone. But we shall have to find nearer at hand some way to meet this need, so we suggest in the absence of the tree trunk, or a shaping block that you take a two-quart fruit jar, place a rounded, medium sized bowl over the top of the jar, placing your flat placque over the bottom of the bowl, hold-

Bam-tush Basket.

ing it firmly in place with the palm of the left hand, leaving the *fingers* and *right hand* free to weave. We experimented using the top only of a fruit jar for shaping, which gave us a small, but perfectly modeled basket. We might mention, that it would be well to fill the jar with sand, the added weight helping to keep the jar more firmly in place. It is absolutely necessary that your upright "bams" do not touch the table. They must be free. Should any of your "bams" be pulled out by accident after you have woven them in, take a good-sized knitting needle or a large-sized wire, sharpened to a point (in lieu of the bone stiletto which forms a part of every squaw's weaving paraphernalia,) and open the meshes of weaving so that the "bam" may be returned to its place.

A Section of Chu-set Bowl.

The question may be asked, and a reasonable one, too,—"What size ought the flat placque to be woven before shaping?" This will depend largely upon the shape you wish to have your basket. For fifteen-inch length "bams" and for the shaped basket given to illustrate this lesson, the bottom of the placque should be three inches in diameter before shaping. Should the worker desire a more shallow flat basket, the placque must be woven larger. As we have said before, this is largely individual.

In shaping *add* "bams" to make the basket larger, or to give the desired swell, or peculiarly beautiful roundness which make a "bam-tush" basket such a joy to its possessor. To draw in or make *smaller* at the top, cut the "bams" out as is needed to give the desired shape.

TO FINISH OFF TOP OF THE BASKET.

Thoroughly wet the edges and leave over night, or until abso-

Enlarged Section of a Bam-tush, showing the Uncut Ends of Bams for the Finishing Off of the Basket.

Bottom of Finished Bam-tush.

lutely dry. Then take a sharp knife and trim off the ends of the "bams" about half or a little less than a half inch above the weaving. Also trim off the loose ends inside of the basket. This may seem a careless manner of treating the top, but it seems to be substantial, and a method always followed by the Pomo Indians. Wetting the raphia brings out a gummy substance which after it is dried, seems to set it so that it holds its place.

80

Handsome Specimens of Pomo Burden Baskets.

A Large Granary Basket, 4 feet, 9 inches in height.

Pomo Indian Burden Basket of Bam-tush Weave.

WEAVING THE "TI" BAND.

The Pomo Indians use this "Ti" to strengthen, as well as beautify, their baskets. This is a difficult part of an upright weave, but once understood, is quite an acquisition to the worker's knowledge of Indian Basketry.

We hope with the accompanying illustration, and by using the letters A, B, C, D, to explain in a very simple manner the technic of this part of the work, using the letters to name the different elements used. (A) stands for the upright "bams" or *warp*. (B) a horizontal "bam" crossing these at right angles, while (C and D) are the weaving threads of raphia. By examining very carefully, the worker will see that the "Ti" band is a regular plain twined weaving, holding the *upright* and horizontal bands together.

The *inside* of the basket presents the same appearance that the plain twined, or Bam-Tush basket gives, while the *outside* differs greatly. The *upright* "bams" may be of No. 1, 2 or 3 reeds, as the worker prefers, but the "*ti*"-*band* must be correspondingly smaller, say a No. "oo," the smallest reed made, or a hard, twisted thread of raphia. Often the Indians use a coarse brown cord, made from the hemp mixed with other plant fibers, in place of the willow "bam."

After the flat placque has been woven about three inches in diameter (supposing that the worker has decided to have "ti" bands upon the "bam-tush" and that we are using the same dimensions in regard to size of basket) see that the weaving threads upon your placque are long; if they are short, add in new ones, weaving enough to be quite sure that they are fastened securely.

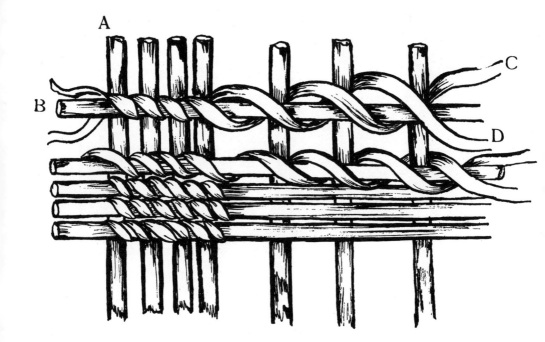

Illustrating the method of weaving the " Ti " Band by the Pomos.

Take your placque, see that the weaving threads lay upon the right hand side, as it lays flat upon a table. Have ready the "ti" band. Place one end upon your placque, pushing one inch of the band to the inside (under the placque) having the bent part of the "ti" band, where it is pushed under the placque, and the weaving threads come *together*. Hold the placque with the fingers of the right hand, commence weaving with the threads (C and D), bringing (C) over the "bams" (A and B) as they lay at right angles, while (D) goes *under* and *back* of the (A and B) "bams." Now (C) crosses *under* and *back* while (D) comes over to the *outside;* (C and D) cross each other as in the plain twined weaving, first one and then the other. Always be careful to have the "ti" band held firmly in place, and see that it *follows* the *curve* of the basket, keeping close to the preceding rows of weaving.

Should the worker desire only a narrow band of this weaving, say four or five rows, we would advise putting it on in solid color, which is very effective. As the "ti" weaving progresses, add in the needed upright (A and B) "bams."

Always weave so that the end of the "ti" band may be cut off, and an inch end of the same pushed *under opposite* the starting point; this will give an even band of color. Should the worker desire only *one* row of this weaving, carry the "ti" band a little past the starting point to insure its being held firmly in place. This is for the "ti" band made of the twisted raphia, or heavy cord. The rattan or reed "ti" band is *commenced* by simply laying it upon the outside, (not pushing under the placque), and weaving in exactly as we do the soft "ti" band.

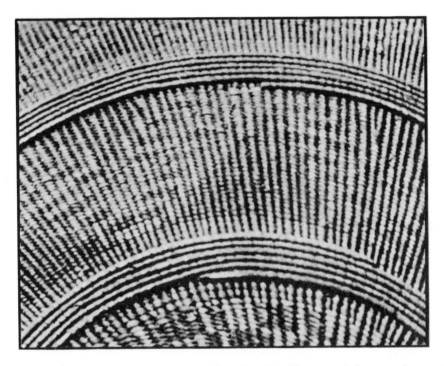

Enlarged Section of a " Ti " Basket Showing the Manner of Commencing and Finishing the " Ti " Band.

To *finish* the reed "ti" band, cut it off squarely, but do not attempt to push this under the placque. After this has been done, continue the plain twined weaving, adding as many rows of "ti" weaving as the worker desires.

The Pomo Indians have given us some magnificent specimens of the "ti" weaving. The group in our collection of carrying or burden baskets, gives but a faint idea of the size, and splendor of coloring as well as design. These baskets are entirely woven after this style, and are called "Ti" baskets.

Dr. Hudson in his writings upon basketry calls them "Tee" baskets, but "tee" and "ti" are really the same.

THREE-PLY TWINED WEAVING.

Many pleasing varieties of this most primitve mode of weaving are found among many Indian tribes. Some fine specimens have been found in the ancient mounds of the Mississippi Valley, also in the Rocky Mountains, and down the Pacific Coast from Attu Island, the most westerly of the Aleutian group, on to Chile; while scattered through different portions of the Atlantic slope of South America may be found some of the most delicate and intricately woven examples of *twined* basketry.

We find beside the plain twine, using two threads or weft element,
The Three-ply Twine,
The Three-ply Embroidery of
The Tlinkit Indians
The Frapped Skokomish
which all belong to the upright twined weaves.

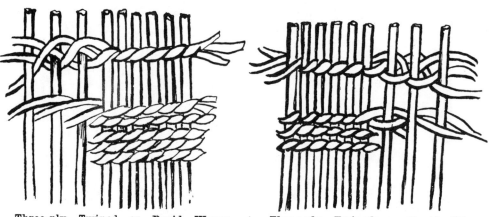

Three-ply Twined or Braid Weave,   Three-ply Twined or Braid Weave,
Outside.   Inside.

CROSSED WARP TWINED WEAVING OF THE MAKAH INDIANS, WASHINGTON STATE.

We are indebted to the Makah Indians of Washington State for a good example of hexagonal weaving. They use this very effectively in the weaving of wallets, letter-cases, or envelope-shaped baskets for holding photographs and postal cards. Quite attractive and saleable are the bottles, covered with this weaving.

While it would be hardly possible to get the bast of hemp which the Makah Indians use so largely in their weaving, some good results may be obtained by using splints with Sweet Grass, colored or natural raphia for the weaving threads.

To cover a bottle with this hexagonal weaving, commence at the bottom; have the upright splints radiate from the center, bringing every other upright splint to the *right* hand, crossing over the next one, which is brought to the *left* hand. After crossing, the splints are held in place by a row of twined weaving, either of sweet grass or raphia. A good way to measure the length of splints, (or raphia used in place of splints) is to allow for the *length* twice and a half as long as the bottle to be covered, or the basket to be woven.

Crossed Warp Twined Weaving of the Makah Indians.

For the width, there should be as many splints as, when laid side by side close together, will make the width desired. To shape in around the neck of the bottle is very simple. Draw the splints over so that the meshes become smaller, and some of the splints are woven in double, that is, they are placed one over the other.

The worker's artistic sense, coupled with ingenuity, will suggest many charming possibilities in the use of this weave.

A very pretty way to finish off the edge of a basket, where the raphia or sweet grass have been used as the twining threads, is to cut every other upright splint *short,* leaving the others about an inch or three-quarters of an inch above the weaving. These are then thoroughly wet, and bent sharply down inside the basket over a piece of splint which is fitted around inside the rim of the basket, with its ends overlapping. A second splint is laid over this to cover the splint ends inside of the basket, while a braided rope of raphia or sweet grass is laid around the *outside.*

A twining thread is then started close to the edge and *sewed* over and over, passing between the upright splints and holding the inside splint, and the outside braid firmly in place. A cover may be made just large enough to fit over the basket, and finished off in the same way.

BIRD-CAGE WEAVE.

The bird cage twine of the Clallam and Makah Indians make a pleasing variety for a collection of baskets. This may be woven with fine or coarse reeds, as the worker desires, and may be woven with quite an open mesh, or the rows of twining placed close together.

To duplicate the open-meshed weave, given in cut No. 23, use No. 5 rattan for the upright "bam," or spokes, No. 3 rattan for the horizontal "bam" and raphia (a single leaf) for the twining element. The horizontal reed or "bam" is laid *back* of the upright "bams," while the raphia binds the upright and horizontal "bams" together where they *cross* each other. The rows of twining are about an inch apart.

Wrapped twined weaving, using only one strand of

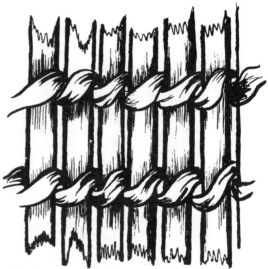

Bird Cage Twined Weave, by the Makah and Clallam Indians.

raphia, which is pushed up close to the preceding row of weaving, as in the bird-cage weave, gives an unusual but attractive surface.

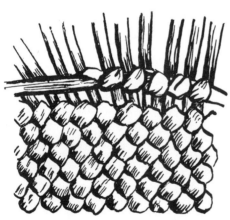

Wrapped Twined Weaving.

TLINKIT BASKETRY OR INDIAN EMBROIDERY.

In Tlinkit Basketry, the body of the basket is worked in spruce root, which gives an exceedingly tough fiber, well suited for this especial kind of weaving in the different designs which ornament many of these baskets. These designs contain many symbols of a mythological character, making every line upon an Indian basket eloquent with meaning, could we fully understand and interpret them.

In the needle work of the Indian women's white sisters, the working in of this third element would be called embroidery but the squaw twines it into the weaving as the basket progresses. That is, when *each* one of the twining or weaving threads pass between the two upright "bams" or rods *outward,* the colored or overlaid strips of material are wrapped around this twining thread once. Straws of different colors are largely used, and are very effective being capable of splitting into different widths. They must be soaked or dampened in water before using. We have many interesting specimens of this overlaid work, each tribe modifying and changing the process of weaving somewhat, but the general effect is quite similar.

The Frapped Basketry of the Skokomish is somewhat like the Tlinkit overlaying; also among the Pomos we find where this style of basketry has given s o m e splendid s p e c i-mens, they using corn-husks, squaw grass and other materials for the overlay. These baskets are coarse-ly finished off round the top, as nearly all of the upright t w i n e d baskets seem to be. However, they are strong and substantial.

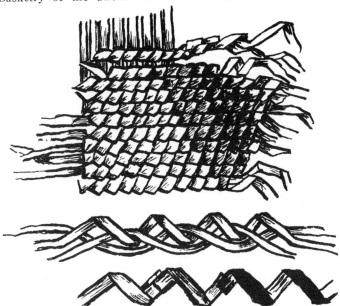

Showing the Overlaid Twining or False Embroidery.

Aleut Basket.

We have also pleasing varieties of this plain twined weaving from the Aleutian Islands. The Aleuts frequently use for their upright warp or "bams," stems of wild rye or other grasses in which the straws are split in two parts, the two halves passing upward in a zig-zag manner; each half of one of these straws or warp being fastened alternately with the other half of the same straw and with a half of an adjoining straw, making a series of regularly shaped openings. Raphia or sweet grass could be used to advantage as the twining threads.

DIAGONAL WEAVING.

The technic of this weave lies in the passing over *two* or more "bams" at each half turn; for in the next round of weaving the same pairs of "bams" are not included in the half turns, so the worker

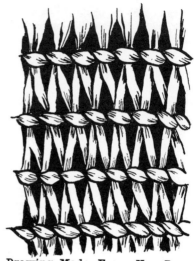

Drawing Made From Nez Perce Letter Case.

Showing a Portion of Twined Weaving From a Hopi Water Bottle.

Showing a Portion of "Ute" Basket, Giving Diagonal Weave.

must be sure of having an added number of "bams."

This weave is used among the Apaches, as well as the Utes, who dip the bottles made in this fashion into pitch and thus make a water-tight vessel, the very open meshes of weaving receiving the pitch more freely than some of the more closely woven weaves.

BASKETS MADE FROM THE DATE AND FAN PALMS

To the many tourists who visit in the different parts of semi-tropical portions of this country, we wish to make some suggestions for the weaving of charming baskets from the Date and Fan Palm leaves.

Illustration No. 1—Finished Basket Woven from Fan Palm.

After weaving one or two of these baskets the worker will find many original ways of shaping and weaving this product of nature into dainty little bon-bon boxes, flat tray baskets for holding nuts or fruit, waste paper baskets, jardineires, and from the Fan Palm we have seen exceptionally pretty cases for toilet use, lined in with silk and tufted with cotton underneath.

Baskets made from these are strong and durable, keeping their shapes admirably. As they dry they seem to grow more beautiful in coloring, the deep green changing to a soft grey sage green. The drying process seems to give a somewhat glazed surface to the baskets woven from the Date Palm that is very artistic.

However, if one wished to keep the deep, natural green of the fresh leaves, give a surface covering by using a shellac finish of one part white shellac to thirty (30) parts of wood alcohol. This can be bought at any paint store. Apply with a soft brush as one would varnish. Leave the basket in some cool, dark place away from the dust until it has thoroughly dried. When we say to dry, this means the basket itself as well as the shellac finish, for of course being woven from the fresh green, it is necessary that it be allowed time to dry and shape.

PREPARING THE FAN PALM.

Select a large sized fresh Fan Palm leaf. Wash thoroughly with garden hose, freeing it from dust, wipe dry and with a sharp knife cut the green from the stem, cutting close to the stem, so that the green strips may be as long as possible.

Take a pair of sharp shears, and cut the green into one-half inch strips. These strips must be cut

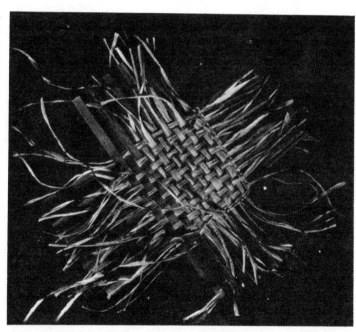

Cut No. 2—Showing the Manner of Commencing the Bottom of the Basket.

evenly; keep them damp by laying between damp cloth.

To weave the basket in illustration No. 1, required strips of green thirty-two inches long, also natural raphia the same length. This basket is square, measuring seven inches each way, and is eleven and one-half inches tall. Lay eleven of these flat upon the table weaving in the other eleven forming a seven-inch square of weaving in the center of these 32 inch strips of green.

We turn these ends up and weave them for the sides, so that it is absolutely necessary that the square of weaving which forms the bottom be kept in the center of the weavers.

When the square is woven, thread a No. 19 tapestry needle with a large thread of raphia (natural) and weave in on top of the green strips. This is easier than to weave them in at the time the strips are woven.

Cut No. 2 fully illustrates the above directions.

After the raphia has been woven into the bottom, and the square of weaving pushed up closely and firmly together, take two threads of raphia and weave a row of pairing around the square. This is to hold the raphia and palm strips in place. The bottom is now ready for the sides. Cut each palm strip up the center, that is, divide each into equal parts. Take the same raphia pairing threads (if long enough, if not, add in new thread and weave or pair with both *old* and *new* thread for two or three inches, then push the end of old thread to the inside of the basket to be trimmed off later,) and weave a second row of pairing, keeping the raphia threads, which were woven in with the palms, to a regular place, that is, one-half of the cut palm green would be without a raphia thread.

Cut No. 2 shows the two rows of pairing, and also the way the raphia is placed.

TURNING THE SIDES.

To turn the sides for weaving, take a box the *same size* square as the weaving, and shape the sides down squarely over it. Please carefully examine Illustration No. 3. The worker will then understand what is meant by the request that they take one of the green palm strips and weave it horizontally over and under the divided upright strips, always leaving the strip of green palm with its corresponding strip or thread of raphia upon the *outside* of the basket, while the other divided half of the strip goes *under* and *inside*. When adding in a new horizontal strip of green palm carry one end three or four inches over the other end, and this will be sufficient to hold it in place. Cutting off the end outside, it will slip back *under* the weaving and not show.

Each row is finished off by itself differing from the continuous coil basket which is an ascending spiral. When adding in each new horizontal strip of green the weaving or pairing threads cross each other always at the same corner and are thus carried up for the new row of pairing. The corner which shows so clearly in illustration No. 3 shows the method of crossing the thread. It is optional with the worker as to the size or shape of the basket; it may be flat or tall, but some pleasing results may be gained by originating new shapes and using different colored raphia for the weaving element.

TO FINISH TOP.

When enough of the basket has been woven to please the worker, finish off the top by turning the divided half of the upright green strip which has always been woven in with the raphia down *over* the edge, or last row of pairing, and pushing them under the weaving threads inside of the basket.

This will leave the upright raphia thread, and the other divided half of the upright strip of green to be finished off with the second row of pairing or weaving, as each pairing or turn is taken, pull the upright raphia *over* to the inside of the basket just as if one intended to braid it in, but only give it one turn, and then go on weaving in the upright palm strips leaving them standing upright until the weaving of the raphia has been finished; then turn these upright palm strips *over* the edge, and weave them under the raphia threads upon the *inside* of the basket.

Cut off the ends of the turned in upright raphia threads, leaving them about one-half inch long; this makes a very pretty artistic finish, not at all objectionable. The pairing or weaving threads tie securely and draw the ends under some of the weaving stitches *inside* the basket, cutting them off.

Illustration No. 3. Fan Palm Basket, Showing the Basket After the Sides Have Been Turned for Weaving.

DATE-PALM BASKET.

For a small waste-paper basket, eight or nine inches tall, cut the tip ends of your date palm branches, counting the length of the mid-rib for the measurement, *after* cutting off three or four inches of the tip end of the leaf. The

Illustration No. 3—Date-Palm Baskets.

two baskets in illustration No. 3 can be made from four leaves, using the tips of the leaves for the smaller basket, and the larger and heavier center portion for the tall basket, which measures twenty inches for the mid-rib, six inches at bottom (which is square), and nine inches for the top and gives good proportions and balance.

Illustration No. 1—Date-Palm Basket.

PREPARING THE LEAVES.

Thoroughly wash the leaves with a garden hose, this freshens them, removing the dust, as well as making it easier to manage. When cutting the midrib, be sure and see that it is cut squarely off at the bottom so that the basket

Illustration No. 2. Date Palm Basket, Showing the Numbered
Strips Which Are Added to Complete the Bottom.

may stand firmly, and that there shall be the *same number of leaves,* and that these leaves shall come *opposite* each other for the weaving.

WEAVING.

When ready to weave, place two leaves together flat upon a table and weave them together as in cut No. 1; of the four leaves make two such sides, before joining them together. Weave these leaves over and under, holding the weaving in place by turning each leaf back upon itself, and weaving it under. After the basket has been thoroughly dried, these ends are cut off, where they slip under a cross weave and thus are hidden. One-half can come upon the inside of the basket and the other half upon the outside. When the four sides have been woven and the joining made, finish off the top or points, which must be woven before the bottom is finished. Keep the leaves of the palm thoroughly dampened so they may be bent over sharply without breaking, or splitting. Should any delay occur while weaving this basket, keep it covered with a wet cloth and stand in a cool place.

TO FINISH BOTTOM.

The Date Palm has short leaves, which fold together and which do not give long enough weavers to finish the bottom of this basket, so we cut from the Fan Palm the same width weavers as the leaves of the Date Palm in the partially woven basket. Please carefully examine illustration No. 2. The numbered weavers, 1, 2, 3, and 4 are from the Fan Palm, and are woven in, over and under just as the sides are woven; the ends are turned back, each upon itself to hold it firmly.

Illustration No. 2 is so clear that a further description seems needless. We can assure the worker that a Palm basket is not difficult to make, and will more than repay the labor expended, as well as giving variety to a collection of baskets.

CONTINUOUS COIL BASKET WOVEN FROM PALM FIBRES

Cut the Fan Palm into small strips, say one-fourth of an inch wide, and place six or seven of these strips together to form the coil adding them in as they are needed to keep the coil uniform. The weaving element may be of different colored raphias or quite an Indian effect may be obtained by using the smallest size cane (such as is used for re-seating chairs), for the weaving element. This method of weaving requires an awl or a steel or bone stiletto

Fan Palm Basket, Using No. 1 Cane for the Weaving Thread, and Split Palm Fibres For the Coil.

to open the fibres so that the cane may easily pass through the coil and *under* the stitch below. The coils of palm fibres are not covered twice as in the raphia weaving, but each cane stitch interlocks into the stitch below it, making a strong durable basket.

PINE NEEDLES.

Dainty baskets may be woven by using pine needles for the filling in a continuous coil, adding a few pine needles at a time, so that the size of the coil may be kept uniform. This with the natural or colored raphia thread for the weaving will give a very pretty effect by letting the weaving run spirally from the bottom to the top, keeping these spirals one-half inch apart, showing the pine needles through.

BASKETS FROM RICE STEMS.

Unweave Japanese matting (any matting will do,) take the uncolored grass and tie into small bunches, putting them into plenty of cold water to soak over night. This will soften, and freshen them. Take out of the water and hang up to

Palm Basket.

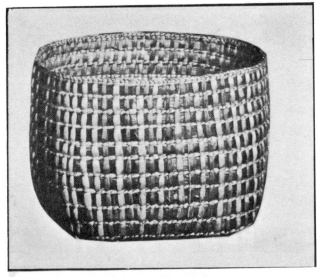

Basket Made From Split Corn-Stalks, These Color Beautifully and are Easily Dyed.

dry and drain thoroughly.

The worker will find these rice straws make an admirable filling for a continuous coil basket or table mats.

Purposely start with uneven ends, the coil is commenced in exactly the same manner that the General Direction give, so that as the coil needs the addition of new stems to keep it uniform they may be added without showing unevenness.

Lay the ends of the new stems in the center of the coil, and slightly roll or twist the coil as the weaving progresses. Weave with very open meshes, showing the rice stems between.

The Hopi Indians weave many of their baskets in this manner making the coils very large, and covering with colored weaving threads.

Some splendid colors may often times be found in remnants of matting, which unwoven would give some good results in the use of a solid color.

RECIPES FOR DYEING RAPHIA.

A word in regard to the coloring, or dyeing, the raphia. We advocate most emphatically the use of vegetable dyes. Dealers in dye-woods and bark can supply nearly all the vegetable extracts for the different colors. The dyes are not hard to manage. In this fascinating part of basketry, a worker may find in the blossoms and roots of plants most desirable shades. One will be surprised to find in the purple iris and roots, a good purple, the blossoms being full of liquid. We give a few suggestions, with the hope that others may find in this part of basketry the same pleasure that we have and that some good results may be gained in further experimenting with the vegetable dyes.

CAUTION.

In dyeing the raphia *never boil,* but bring up to the boiling point and keep there the time required. Boiling or keeping at too great degree of heat will burn or rot the raphia.

In asking for fustic, be sure and ask for old fustic, as the young fustic is quite a different article, and when a recipe calls for fustic alone, it means old fustic. A pound of extract of logwood is equal to four pounds of logwood chips.

TO COLOR WOOD BROWN.

For dyeing ten pounds of raphia, boil two pounds fustic and four pounds cam-wood, *one* hour, and if too light color, add one-tenth pound each of copperas and alum to darken.

BLUE.

Put two and one-half pounds copperas in fifteen gallons water; let dissolve. Put in this solution ten pounds raphia, and *simmer* (not *boil*) two hours, then take out and rinse in clear water. Refill kettle with clear water and add one-half pound prussiate of potash. Simmer in this solution three-quarters of an hour, then lift the raphia out of this, and slowly add to the remaining solution one-half pound oil of vitriol; return the raphia and simmer three-quarters of an hour longer, then rinse thoroughly in clear water.

TO COLOR GREEN.

Add eight pounds fustic, and one-half pound alum to the blue of the preceding rule, put in raphia and simmer until the required shade of green is obtained.

Experience will show the worker that many gradations of color can be made from the above recipes by allowing the raphia to remain a shorter or longer time in the dye-bath.

Be sure after dyeing that the raphia is *thoroughly dried,* to prevent mildew and rotting.

YELLOW.

Before the raphia is dyed, soak it over night in a mordant or fixing bath made of 3 oz. alum, dissolved in one quart of water. If fustic chips are used, soak them over night in water enough to cover them, and then boil in the same water fifteen or twenty minutes, or long enough to give a bright yellow color. From time to time, dip a bit of raphia in the dye to try the color, and as soon as it dyes a bright yellow, remove the dye from the fire and strain; it is then ready for use. Longer boiling gives the duller olive shades. Extract of fustic gives surer results with less labor. If this is used, dilute with hot water. Cochineal added to the fustic gives a dull red orange.

BLACK.

Boil logwood chips in water enough to cover them for fifteen or twenty minutes. Soak the raphia in a solution composed of fifty (50) parts of logwood and ten (10) parts of fustic for one-half hour. Then remove the raphia and add to the solution four parts of copperas, returning the raphia for fifteen or twenty minutes. This gives a good black.

SCARLET.

Mordant the raphia with six parts of stannous chloride crystals and four parts of cream of tartar. Boil cochineal and strain, dyeing the raphia until the desired color is obtained.

PURPLE.

Use the alum mordant as in the yellow. Dye raphia a soft purple by soaking for a time in extract of logwood obtained by boiling the chips; adding ammonia or baking powder gives a bluer purple.

ORANGE.

The properties of quercitron are very much like those of fustic, but used with a mordant of stannous chloride, its yellow partakes more of the orange than the fustic colors. Make a solution of stannous chloride and mordant the raphia. Dilute extract of quercitron with boiling water. It is then ready for use.

BROWN.

Boiling logwood chips in water enough to cover them for fifteen or twenty minutes, gives a yellow brown color. Soak the raphia in this color for a time, using no mordant, and then dry.

BOTTLE GREEN.

To color Bottle Green, for a mordant or fixer, make a boiling solution of one-tenth of a pound of chrome and one-fifth of a pound of alum. Dip the raphia in and thoroughly wet it. Take it out and have another vessel of boiling solution of three pounds of fustic and one and one-half pounds of logwood; put in the raphia, saturating thoroughly in the liquid. This amount makes a dye for ten pounds of material; lessen the amount acccording to the need.

POLISH AND WOOD STAINS FOR RATTANS.

Reeds or rattans being a product of wood, the use of wood stains would seem very appropriate. There are many people who prefer the natural color of the reeds, but do not care for the dull unfinished appearance of the reeds as they are woven.

For those who prefer the reeds in their natural color, we give the two following recipes:

The polish acts like a varnish, while it stiffens the rattan making it somewhat deeper and more yellow in tone, and does not give the surface an objectionable shine. Usually the polish and stains are applied to the finished basket with a brush. This applies to the baskets woven *entirely* of reeds; but when *other weaving* elements enter into the problem, it can be seen at a glance the utter impossibility of successfully staining or polishing a basket so woven.

Hence our suggestion for the worker to stain or polish the reeds *before* weaving.

Take four or five lengths of reed, tying them together firmly at one end, suspending them from a nail driven as high up as one can conveniently reach. Hold the reeds in the left hand, and apply the stain or polish with the right, using a stiff bristle brush. After the reeds are dried, any roughness may be removed by polishing with an emery paper, or No. " oo " sand paper. Often one can get for the asking sheets of old sand paper, which have been removed from the planer at some planing mill; these are useless for further work, but answer admirably for taking the roughness from shellacked or polished surfaces. Do not use the sand paper too vigorously, as very little rubbing is all that is necessary.

POLISH.

Take *equal* parts of Light Oil Finish (known commercially by this name) and turpentine; mix thoroughly and apply with a stiff paint brush. If it is impossible to obtain this varnish known as Light Oil Finish, a common copal and turpentine varnish may be used. This will require two parts of turpentine to one of varnish. When dry, sand-paper.

DEEPER OIL FINISH.

Take *two* parts of turpentine to *four* parts of linseed oil, and *one* part of cherry stain; thoroughly mix, and rub well into the rattan. This gives a considerably darker finish.

PALE OIL FINISH.

This makes the rattan smooth and glossy, slightly darker than the natural color. Mix thoroughly *one* part of turpentine to *three* parts of linseed oil. Rub this into the rattans with a soft cloth. It takes considerably longer for this finish to dry, but it is very artistic.

GREEN OIL FINISH.

A beautiful yellow green with life and brilliancy is made with *twelve* parts of turpentine to *nine* parts of linseed oil and Malachite Green stain added drop by drop until the desired shade is secured.

A very dainty pale shade of green is obtained by adding a few drops of Malachite Green stain to *twenty-one* parts of turpentine and *five* parts of Light Oil Finish. This does not have so decided a polish, owing to the larger amount of turpentine used, but many prefer the pale silvery effect. It is wise to test your color upon a small piece of rattan before finishing the needed quantity of reeds.

A DEEPER GREEN POLISH.

To equal parts of Light Oil Finish and turpentine, add a small quantity of Malachite Green; carefully test for the shade, by adding a drop at a time and trying the color upon a piece of rattan.

OLIVE GREEN POLISH.

Add drop by drop Green Oak Stain to *equal* parts of turpentine and Light Oil Finish, testing upon a piece of reed until the right shade has been obtained.

TERRA COTTA POLISH

Is made by adding to *one* part of Light Oil Finish, and *two* parts of turpentine, cherry stain. This needs only a few drops to give the desired shade.

ORANGE STAIN.

Purchase at any drug store a small quantity of Wood Alcohol, also a stick of Dragon's Blood. This is used by musical instrument makers to color their varnishes, and when ground in alcohol gives a beautiful orange red. By the addition of different colored stains to certain combinations of turpentine and linseed oil, or turpentine and varnish, some splendid results may be obtained, and the worker well repaid for the time expended in experimenting.

Take for an example, *five* parts of Light Oil Finish and *twenty-one* parts of turpentine; add a few drops of cherry stain or enough to give a deep terra cotta color, which is very much like an Indian Red, and when used with black in weaving gives a good color scheme.

DYEING THE REEDS

In coloring the reeds, follow exactly the directions given for dyeing raphia, testing carefully with a small piece of rattan, which has been soaked in the mordant or fixing bath, should the recipe call for such a bath.

These recipes are given for vegetable dyes, and will more than repay the worker for the time and trouble. The reeds will give soft artistic shades and lasting colors,—results that cannot be obtained by using the analine dyes.

A Choice Collection of California Baskets.